PRAISE FOR *HIGH HEELS*
IN THE LAUNDRY ROOM

"Michelle's drive is contagious and will empower
women and girls to think bigger!"

CARA BELVIN, FOUNDER OF EMPOWERHER

HIGH HEELS IN THE
LAUNDRY ROOM

MICHELLE CULLY

High Heels in the Laundry Room

How I Faced Fear,
Found My Voice, and Built
a Business on My Terms

ISBN 978-1-7325706-0-3 (print)
ISBN 978-1-7325706-1-0 (ebook)

Some names and identifying details have been changed
to protect the privacy of individuals.

Produced by Page Two
www.pagetwostrategies.com
Cover design by Taysia Louie
Cover photo courtesy Kerry Brett
Interior design by Taysia Louie
and Prateeba Perumal

Printed and bound in Canada by Island Blue

18 19 20 21   5 4 3 2 1

www.michellecully.com

To anyone who has been told they aren't good enough,
I hope that by reading this book, you find yourself.

CONTENTS

_____

PREFACE

In may 2017, I was honored to give the commencement speech for the graduating class of the New England College of Business and Finance. I was crazy nervous. This was the first college graduation I'd ever attended. In fact, I'd never set foot on a college campus until that moment. Well, that isn't entirely true. I'm pretty sure I'd delivered a package or two to some college building or other—a shipment of textbooks, maybe some science equipment that weighed a ton. But take a class, that's something I'd never done.

I looked out at the audience—row upon row of smiling faces; gowns; flat, square caps with tassels; proud parents snapping photos—and took a step away from the microphone. The audience members gazed back at me expectantly.

Really, I had no right to be there. I'd spent the previous two decades embarrassed whenever the conversation turned to everyone's college experience, the big-name schools they'd attended, how far they'd come because of it, and where they could go thanks to their degrees. You want to key into my insecurities, my constant need for reassurance, just bring up my missing college degree. Some things you never outgrow.

I had no right to be there because I was that girl no one ever expects to recover from her mistakes; that girl from a nice, normal family who somehow got in way over her head and never quite went anywhere. The one who lies about her black eyes, puts in ninety hours a week working for an abusive boyfriend, and is completely isolated from her friends and family. The girl who can't pee without her boyfriend telling her she pees too loudly; who can't take a shower with the curtain closed because every time she turns her back, he changes the water to scalding.

A graduate in the front row, blond, tiny like me, leaned back in her chair and waited for me to begin. She couldn't have been more than a couple of years older than my daughter. The young man beside her put his arm around her. I wondered if he was a sweet boy, like my son, or someone you'd want to watch out for. I pulled myself out of my thoughts and remembered why I was there. I began speaking, tentatively at first.

"As I look out at all of you today, I've got to say, I admire your tenacity, hard work, and the commitment that it's taken to get you to where you're sitting today. My hope is that my story will empower all of you to write your own story as you finish this chapter and continue on."

I may not have a framed degree hanging on my wall, but what I do have is a business that is all mine. I didn't pay tuition for the lessons my business taught me—well, that's a lie, I pay for them every day, and let me tell you, I've sacrificed a lot for them—but that education was the reason I was giving a speech. I have a wildly successful business, one I started with my own hands—and that business helped me make something of myself against all the odds. That business saved me from myself.

"I'm in the trucking business. Yes, trucking. I've owned Xpressman Trucking and Courier, Inc. since 1993." I looked around the auditorium and realized that I had everyone's attention. No one expects a 100-pound woman in expensive high heels and a short skirt to head a trucking company. I should be a cosmetic sales rep or a talk show host. Looks aside, don't get me started on my complete inability to find my way out of a paper bag. It's still one of the best running jokes among those who know and love me. Simply put, I can't manoeuver from point A to point B without getting lost, which is tough when you deal in logistics. I have a GPS in each of my vehicles. I do MapQuest, complete with printouts. I would carry atlases, radar equipment, even a divining rod in my trunk if they would help. If I want to get somewhere I don't know well, I have to stay on the phone with my dispatchers each and every time, because I can't find my way around without their help. It's kind of funny how dependent I still am, and how much I've had to learn about myself in order to be able to laugh in such situations.

"I built Xpressman from necessity, from hard work, and from sheer determination. Not bad for someone who was told, 'You'll never amount to anything.' Who believed it."

The room grew quiet. I had every person's attention. It still takes me by surprise when people react that way.

"I never set out to be an entrepreneur." Apparently, I'm an entrepreneur. It's funny for me to say those words because I think of an entrepreneur as someone with multiple companies, $50 million in the bank, and a summer home. Am I really an entrepreneur? I know that I am because I started my business by myself. I worked insanely hard to take it to where it is today. I make a comfortable living. I've made a nice life for myself and my family. I've even started another company, in real estate development. So, yes, I'm an entrepreneur. I just don't see myself in that light, because I almost feel as though I'm not worthy to be called that. On top of which, I'm always afraid I'm going to lose what I have. I work so hard, and I fear that one day I'm going to wake up and it's going to all be gone, or someone's going to take it away from me, or I'm going to lose every client overnight. Even though, logically, I know I won't let that happen.

"Actually, I was never truly sure what I was going to be. What I did know was that when I was sixteen I fell in love and I was quite content to be with my boyfriend. And for many years, he was my world."

The blond girl in the front row raised an eyebrow. I've got this sixth sense, and sometimes I just know who needs to hear this story, who it might save. I proceeded to direct the rest of my story at her. I told her about my boyfriend; our violent relationship; how I lost my identity; how my family and friends had to pull me away from the wreckage; how I woke up one day and decided to start a company from my parents' laundry room. How naive I was in the beginning, how tenacious I had to be to overcome the endless obstacles, how I learned to eat rejection with a knife and fork. I told her, and all the people in the auditorium, about the self-doubt, how I got taken advantage of, preyed upon, and how others felt sorry for me and helped me out. And that one day, after a lot of sleepless nights and grinding work, I realized that I could rely on myself, that I had the thing by the tail, and that it felt amazing. I told her everything, the good, the bad, and the ugly. Then I drove the point home.

"Today, I have well over a hundred employees and drivers. I own a 33,000-square-foot commercial warehouse building. Xpressman serves customers coast to coast. As I said, I never went to college. I never had a degree to help me navigate the business world."

We are all inspired by success. But here's what you've got to keep in mind: Even though someone may appear very successful, everybody's got their vulnerabilities, challenges, and issues they're working through. Everyone has had to learn life lessons, usually the hard way. It's great to be inspired by something they've done, but it's also important to realize that they're human just like you, that they have insecurities too. Not everything about their life is perfect. When we keep that in mind, we can be a lot kinder to ourselves as we go through our own challenges and reach for our own goals. We tend to be way too hard on ourselves and put ourselves down, which only limits us from taking the action that we really want to take. I had so many lessons I wanted to share with the audience—not just business lessons but personal lessons too, because they're all intertwined. Someone once said that business problems are personal problems in disguise, but I think that personal problems are business opportunities in disguise.

"I believe things happen for a reason, that we're given a path and it's up to us to decide how to handle it, to make that path what we want it to be. What may not make sense today will make sense later. You control your own destiny, you can be as successful as you want to be, but it's up to you to make that happen. No high school diploma? No problem. Disability? Let's see where you fit in. Willing to work hard? Welcome to the team. Each one of you has a place in this world. Each one of you will face challenges. Face them head-on and believe you have the strength to turn adversity into opportunity."

When I looked up from my notes, the audience was clapping. I could hear someone saying, "Ooh, wow. Wow." People were staring at me as though I was a mini-superstar. It was funny, because the last word I would ever use to describe myself is "superstar." Far from it.

"Congratulations, graduates," I said, realizing that I should probably end on a high note.

At the close of the ceremony, a group of women approached me. "What a great story," the boldest one said. "You need to write a book. I wish my youngest daughter had come. You would be such an inspiration to her. She's all caught up with some guy."

"Me? Oh my goodness, that's so sweet."

If they'd only met me twenty-five years earlier.

{ 1 }

THIS IS HOW
IT HAPPENS

WE PULL INTO the restaurant parking lot and circle for a free spot. I continue to sob quietly in the passenger seat. I feel at my scalp where Geoff ripped my hair clean out, and I wince. I have no idea what might happen next. We are supposed to meet friends for dinner, a much older couple in their forties, the sort Geoff has a penchant for hanging around with, but I can't imagine how I can walk in there as if nothing has happened. My eyes are bloodshot and my face is covered in snot. Try as I might, I can't pull myself together.

Geoff had picked me up in his latest fancy car, a bright-red Mustang, and we were speeding along when we got into a bizarre argument. I was crying about something cruel he'd said to me, when he slammed my head as hard as he could against the window. At first I was in complete shock, so much so that I stopped breathing. When I realized what he'd done, I dropped my head in my hands, shook uncontrollably. Geoff then grabbed hold of the back of my head and tore a fistful of hair clean out. My head jerked back, I screamed in pain, and I wailed hysterically.

Geoff shuts off the ignition, gets out of the car, and comes around to the passenger side. He opens my door and offers his hand to help me out. I can't look him in the face; instead, I stare at my feet. I know that we've just reached a point of no return; I feel that in my gut like a cold, hard fist. I saw the warning signs but chose to ignore them. Now, here we are.

I was sixteen when I fell in love with Geoff. We've spent nearly every waking moment together in the two-years since then. A year older than me, Geoff is that popular guy every girl wants to date and every guy wants to be. We go out for dinner in his impressive car a few times a week, just like we're doing tonight, see the latest movies, hang out with friends. Sometimes we'll drive up north for the weekend, pitch a tent, build a roaring campfire, and down some Bud Lights until long after sunset. He'll make me laugh so hard, there in the dark, under the dense canopy of trees, the skin of stars. That's the thing about Geoff: he's hilarious. He can have a crowd in tears within minutes, even if his humor does have a cruel edge to it.

Another car drives into the packed restaurant lot, parks in a spot at the far end, and shuts off its lights. Geoff picks me up from the passenger seat as if I'm a rag doll and carries me toward the restaurant, like a joke, trying to make me laugh all the way across the lot. I finally stop crying because I have no idea what else to do. If he wants me to laugh, maybe we're okay.

Tall and outgoing, Geoff has his pick of pretty girls. He had dated and slept with over a hundred girls—his sisters' friends, high school girls, older or younger, you name it—before I ever met him. Part of his sex appeal is the brand-new, flashy sports car he drives, a different model he manages to procure every six months or so thanks to his parents, natural ambition, and a penchant for saving money for big purchases. Then there's his charisma, the winning smile, the easy confidence.

We make sense, though, Geoff and I. Who else would ride shotgun with him but the former co-captain of the cheerleaders, the Homecoming Queen? The fact that I was still innocent, that I'd never been intimate with anybody else, appealed to the Don Juan in him. That I was cute and popular, with a tendency to hero-worship, also drew Geoff to me.

The couple we're meeting has already been seated. The waiter shows us over to the table with a flourish. Upon seeing me, my face streaked with tears and runny mascara, the woman, practically old enough to be my mother, asks me if I'm okay. Geoff looks at me and smiles as if nothing untoward has happened. His complete lack of worry or remorse unnerves me. I tell her I have very bad allergies. When she raises an eyebrow and asks, "Are you sure?" I say yes.

The first incidence of physical abuse was small, almost imperceptible, which is how these things start, how you find yourself waking up one day wondering how you got in so far over your head. At a fair, Geoff shoved me hard with no warning. Some guys who happened to be walking past caught me as I fell into them. They hadn't seen what Geoff had done, merely looked up at him when he laughed. The next time, he pinched me on the thigh, leaving what felt like a hot red slice, then covered my face with his hands as if to smother me. When I looked up at him, horrified by what had just happened, by the realization that he wasn't horsing around but testing me in some way, he just sat there with his beer, not saying a word, his face a complete blank. I turned to his friends, two teenaged boys in jeans and T-shirts, who looked momentarily taken aback but then acted as though nothing unusual had happened. I wondered if I'd imagined it all, if I were somehow overreacting. Eighteen-year-old girls, after all, have a flair for drama. This had to be normal, a practical joke that had failed to land, because physical abuse didn't happen to people like me.

I have such low self-esteem, which kills my parents because they've showered us kids with so much love and attention. Sure, they may at times be too opinionated or get involved in our lives more than they should, but we, their children, rely on them so much. When I have a problem, the first people I go to are my parents. They're always there for me, 100 percent of the time. Except there's no way I can go to them with this.

On the drive back to my house after dinner, neither of us mentions what happened, the argument we had, the hair ripped out of my head, or the concern his friend expressed. It's as if he never attacked me, as if it won't happen again. "You need to clean yourself up," he says as he pulls into my parents' driveway. "You look like a fucking mess, per usual."

We weren't dating long when Geoff began criticizing me, subtly at first. "You're too thin," he'd say, even though he'd always told me I was adorable. He started buying me Ensure Plus so I'd gain weight. He'd snap the can open and force me to drink it in front of him, his upper lip curled in disgust. It tasted so bad that I held my nose while I choked it down, doing my best to look as if it was no big deal. All I wanted to do was gain weight so I could please him. Then he said my lips were too fat, especially the bottom one. He said, "You're so ugly. Why can't you be pretty like my younger sister?" His sister wasn't pretty, but for some reason she was the standard he held me to.

My brown hair made me look drab and mousy. My blue eyes were the wrong color. He picked apart everything I wore until I didn't know what he wanted from me. If I dressed down, he called me a slob; if I dressed up, he called me a slut. There was never a happy medium. He tore me to shreds whether we were alone or out in public. He belittled me in front of his family and friends every chance he got, which seemed to excite his sister to no end. She seemed to get off on seeing her brother move in for the kill, demonstrate his dominance, and destroy the weak. Eventually, I assumed I deserved such treatment.

The kitchen light is on in the window, which means my parents are waiting up for me. My mother will be in her bathrobe at the Formica table keeping my father company while he enjoys a late coffee.

It's hard to imagine how someone with such a normal, happy life can lose herself the way I have with Geoff. Of course, it makes a lot more sense when a person grows up with this kind of abuse—when this is what they know life and love to be. But I didn't grow up this way. I have the most amazing family and friends.

My parents would never tolerate the situation were they to know about it. They're hardworking people who've sacrificed everything for their four children. They're determined to give us a home full of love, a great life. When my sister, two brothers, and I were growing up, my dad would be out in the driveway at four o'clock in the morning in a foot of snow shoveling his way out so he could drive to the oil station and pick up his truck, then work until six o'clock at night delivering fuel. He worked all the overtime he could so my mom could stay home and he could put food on our table. He was determined that we would never eat leftovers, that there would be a fresh meal on the table each and every night. He didn't work that hard just to see me accept something less than the best, let alone abuse.

And forget about my mom. She's one tough lady. You don't cross Claire if you know what's good for you. I was in sixth grade when two girls started teasing me at school. They'd come up behind me on the walk home from school and hit me on the back, push on my violin. Not long after I'd cried about it to her, Mom happened to be backing the car out of our driveway when she caught sight of the teasing and bullying. She screeched to a halt, jumped out of the car, and ran over. Pointing her bony finger in the girls' faces, she told them, "Don't you ever touch my daughter again! You leave her alone." Sure enough, they didn't bother me from that point on.

Both of my parents will forbid me to be with Geoff if they learn the truth, and that's what I'm most afraid of. After all, I love him, and breaking up with him is the last thing I want to do.

I kiss Geoff good night, get out of the car, and trudge toward the house.

"Later, cunt," Geoff says, his elbow resting on the car's sill. I push open the front door and go inside.

It doesn't matter if you're a nice girl from a loving family; it can happen to you. But the good news is you can change your direction at any time and choose "you" first.

{ 2 }

SOME CRAZY
HALF-BAKED PLAN

M Y PARENTS HAD just returned from vacation, one they no doubt needed after all the Geoff drama I'd put them through. Again. I walked in their door looking as if I'd just crawled out from under a rock—stick-thin, my brown hair a mess, mascara blotched. This was a few years after Geoff ripped out my hair on our way to the restaurant to meet his friends. I was twenty-three. Geoff and I were off again, and I was out of a job. I'd been camped out at a small apartment that my sister shared with my best friend, Shea; refusing to eat or shower because Geoff had dumped me; going to a therapist— the only one my parents knew of—who specialized in substance abuse, even though that wasn't my "problem." My parents didn't know much about therapists, and this was the only counselor who was referred to us. I was driving around in one of Geoff's cars that I was unable to pay for, which he'd repossess if I didn't figure out how to come up with some money.

My father looked up from his newspaper, cast a conspiratorial glance at my mother. "So, what are you going to do today?" he asked me, all casual like.

Both of my parents wanted to be supportive of me, but they also wanted to know whether I had some semblance of a plan. There was only so long they could stand by as I sank roots into Gina's couch. Now that I was no longer working with Geoff at the sign manufacturing company he'd founded, I had to get a job or go to college; those were the only two choices.

"Well," I said, and I'd honestly given this only a moment's thought on my drive over, "I'm going to open up my own business today."

"Oh?" was their mutual response. They exchanged an incredulous look. Surely their daughter had lost her mind. Maybe she'd suffered, this time, a complete nervous breakdown. I'd come close any number of times.

I repeated myself a little louder, having mustered a bit more confidence. "Yes, I'm opening up my own business today."

My dad raised an eyebrow. "Oh, okay! What kind of business is this?" He appeared to be reaching deep into his reserves of parental positivity. My mother sat beside him on the couch, gripping her knees. She'd been the one to track down a therapist for me; she was no doubt wondering if she'd botched the job.

"I'm going to open up a courier company, and I need to use your laundry room as my office."

My parents' house was a cozy rancher. In order to reach the laundry room, you had to walk through the living room, where my parents were seated, and the kitchen. I was essentially telling them that I intended to take over their house, making it difficult to move an inch without tripping over me and my half-formed-adult misery. They were running a load in the washing machine at that moment. I could smell the bleach and detergent. The spin cycle had begun; the machine thumped and jerked across the linoleum floor. The laundry room was small, but as far as I was concerned it would do.

They looked at each other again, probably assuming I was going through some phase, and said, "That sounds great, Mish." If a business venture, no matter how improbable, could get me back into life, they were going to humor me. What was the harm in me playing businesswoman for a while? At least they could keep me company and watch over me so I wouldn't damage myself any further. At this point, they had no idea of the level of abuse I'd suffered.

My office space secured, the next logical step was to make my way to OfficeMax to buy some supplies. Driving there, I replayed Geoff's words in my head: *You'll never amount to anything without me. You'll never amount to anything without me.* The words had made me weep all the way to Canal Street, until I'd stopped long enough to consider my bizarre idea—and really, it was bizarre. I'd latched on to the first idea that had inexplicably popped into my mind without having the faintest clue if it would be viable, if there was a need for another courier service in the Boston area, if I'd be squashed like a bug by the competition. I mean, what did I know about running a courier company? I could barely find my way around my own neighborhood. All I knew was that we regularly used a variety of courier companies at Geoff's office, so they must be in demand. But now I felt something else: anger. He was done with me, he'd made that abundantly clear. I'd show him who I was on my own. A fresh wave of doubt swept over me, then passed. I felt something new: freedom, and a sense that I needed to succeed at this business so I could prove to myself I was somebody.

At OfficeMax, I looked up and down each aisle, perused the file folders and the manila envelopes, the plastic containers and the packing bubbles, but all I could think of buying was colored paper clips and a notebook. What else did you need for a business? I couldn't pull up a mental picture of the office I'd shared with Geoff at Legacy Signs. There was paper, of course, and a Rolodex, but I'd taken those and thrown them in a box when I'd realized there was no going back—not to Geoff, not to my job. What else had I seen or used? I continued to draw a blank. Yet, for some inexplicable reason, I was obsessed with those colored paper clips. I needed them.

Before I hit the cash register, I tossed a calculator in my nearly empty basket. I still have that calculator, all these years later. It's the only calculator I use and it has become my good luck charm. It is the one thing that has kept me tethered to the day-to-day realities of running a business. It demonstrates that my business idea was not some fantasy, which it could easily have been.

In the parking lot, I placed my package in the passenger seat and contemplated my next move. What else would the owner of a courier company need? I thought about the deliverymen who had visited Legacy and imagined looking them up and down. Of course. I zoomed over to Radio Shack and bought a pager; this *was* the early nineties, after all.

As I turned the car back toward my parents' house, it occurred to me that I needed one more thing.

Upon entering the law office, I told the receptionist, a middle-aged woman with a phone stuck to one ear, "I'm here because I need to be 'incorporated.'" I didn't really know what it meant to be incorporated, but I'd seen the "Inc." at the end of most business names, not just Geoff's, so I assumed I needed it too. Geoff had used this lawyer when starting both the dry cleaner's and Legacy Signs. It made sense that I would use him too.

I was brought into an office and told that someone would be right with me. I glanced around at the potted plants, a Cadillac-sized desk, and a box of tissues on the end table, wondering what I thought I was doing. Naive, inexperienced girls like me didn't just show up at a law office with some half-baked plan. I didn't have a degree, hadn't even gone to college. I had no business skills except what I'd taught myself when working at Legacy. It would be a miracle if the guy even talked to me. Then in walked the lawyer, who said, "So I gather you're here to start a business."

I flashed a big smile. It was pretty nuts to be doing this; exciting, too. If the lawyer was taking me seriously, if he wasn't laughing in my face, maybe what I was proposing wasn't so ludicrous after all. Why not me? My idea felt more official and there was no turning back. "Yes, I am."

"Okay, let's get started," he said. "What are you looking to do?" The man had a pleasant face, which didn't betray the least bit of amusement. What I'd proposed seemed perfectly reasonable to him, as far as I could tell.

"A courier company," I replied. "I'm going to move packages around. And I'm going to do truck work, from here to New York City." The words just poured unbidden from my mouth. I had no idea what I was talking about.

He considered my statement for a moment. "Okay, well, you'll need..." and he listed off all the licenses and permits that were needed for that sort of work.

He fanned each set of documents out on the surface of his desk like an oversized deck of cards. It should have occurred to me that I was in over my head, but I figured I'd get through it all, with or without help. How hard could it be? Sure, Geoff was smart, but I'd done most of the administrative work. I'd run the entire back office.

Then he asked, "What are you going to call your company?"

I was surprised by his question, as I'd only come up with the cockamamie idea a few hours earlier. He pulled out a yellow legal pad and asked me to come up with some options, which he would write down. So I started brainstorming: "Red Cap

Trucking? No. Red Cap Express. No. MD Trucking? Nope." He scribbled as fast as I spoke. "Expressman, without the *E*? Xpressman Trucking and Courier. Yes, that's it."

He nodded and then called to the receptionist to type in the business name on each of the documents on his desk. He left no room for doubt; it was just done.

From the lawyer's office, I drove back to my parents' house— I mean, my new office—with a big grin on my face, not really sure whether to laugh at this crazy idea or just curl up in a ball and die. Besides working at Legacy, I'd had no outside business experience. I'd waited tables, and at the dry cleaner's Geoff had owned I'd hung clothes and made sure the pressing machine worked. In fact, the only real job I'd had before working with Geoff had been a major flop.

Right after graduating from high school, I'd taken a job at the corporate office of Papa Gino's Pizza. I was in purchasing, which made me feel smart and sophisticated. After I'd been in the position three weeks, my boss came in and told me she'd made a mistake, that she didn't think I could handle the job. A wave of shame rose up from my belly, which made me want to throw up in my trash can. Not noticing the look of horror on my face, she then said, "We'll give you two options: one, you can take the job as the receptionist, or two, we'll have to let you go." I ended up taking the receptionist job, even though I thought everyone there would laugh at me for being a dummy or, worse, feel sorry for me. At that desk, I learned how to talk to all kinds of people. I also learned how a receptionist deserves to be treated. These two lessons would serve me well.

Back at my parents' house, I called the phone company to arrange for a line to be installed in the laundry room. I unloaded my new paper clips, notebook, and calculator. Then I sat on top of the small bumper pool table that occupied center stage and asked myself, *What am I going to do?* I sat and sat.

I couldn't believe what I had just done. I played with the paper clips, making a daisy chain three yards long. When I got bored with that, I read a stack of back issues of the *Enquirer*. As I read, I kept thinking, *Oh my God. What am I going to do?* Part of me wanted to run back to the couch at Gina's and hide my head under a pillow. Another part knew there was no way I was going to quit.

A few days later, I got a bill in the mail from my lawyer for $1,000. I didn't know what I had expected from him. Did I think that lawyers worked for free? That he'd charge me a nominal amount because I was so young? I called him, telling him, "I don't know how I'm going to pay this." I sobbed on the line because I didn't know what I had gone and done.

So we arranged a trade: I would make deliveries for him until the bill was paid off. To this day I've used him for my legal work because that's what you do when someone is kind to you, when someone believes in you before it ever occurs to you to believe in yourself.

Three days later, I had my official phone line. Sitting on the pool table, with the washing machine threatening to fling itself across the room, I realized I needed to start calling people if I was ever going to drum up business. *Now what do I do?* I asked myself. And then it hit me: the Yellow Pages! I ran into the kitchen, yanked open one of the cabinets, and found my parents' copy. I dragged it back to the pool table and flipped through it, looking for ink companies. Having dealt with more than a couple of ink companies at Legacy, I knew that ink companies used couriers, so I decided to start with them. I began with the *A*s.

"Hi, my name is Michelle from Xpressman Trucking and Courier and I was wondering if your company uses a same-day delivery service and, if so, could I speak to the person who's in charge." I rattled off my introduction without taking a breath so they wouldn't have time to hang up on me.

In the rare instances I was connected with a decision maker, I said, "Hi, this is Michelle from Xpressman. We're a same-day delivery service and we service all of New England including the Tri-State Area. I have ten drivers and an office staff of five." Of course it was only me, but they couldn't know that. I crossed my fingers, hopped up and down. I wasn't sure what had me more anxious, being called out as a fraud or being taken up on my offer.

Over the next couple of hours, I got a lot of no's, but when I reached the *I*s, I got my first yes. Impressions Plus. "Yes, we would like to use your services."

I stood still for a moment, unsure if I'd heard right, then finished up with the call, doing my level best not to squeal like a seventh-grader. Oh my God!

Mom was cooking dinner, so I called out to her, "Mom! I just got my first customer!" Then, to myself: "Shit! How am I going to make this delivery?"

And just like that, I was in business.

You don't have to know what you're doing; you just have to start.

{ 3 }

ALL MY FAULT

WE'RE COMING HOME from a party and stopped at a red light when Geoff starts flirting with the girls in the car next to us. His window rolled down, his elbow resting on the sill, he says, "Hey there. How about you two come for a ride with me in my car?"

The girl behind the wheel shoots me a look of pity and drives off. I say something about his disrespect, and before I know it he has the back of my head in his palm and slams it into the dashboard as hard as he can, not just once but over and over again. I can hear each thud as my forehead, cheekbones, and nose bounce against the unforgiving surface. Pain shoots down my spine, into my jaw, my fingertips. I can think clearly enough only to wonder if any bones have been broken. "Who the fuck do you think you are, cunt," he says with each slam.

But Geoff isn't done with me. At the stoplight, which has long since turned green, he draws his elbow back then punches me in the side of the head, again and again. Cars whiz by in long red streaks. Someone honks, probably because our car is in the middle of the road. By the time he stops, my face is so swollen I can barely see. I sit still, wondering if it's over, if his rage is spent. He looks straight ahead, his fingers gripping the steering wheel so hard his knuckles go white. "You are fucking disgusting, cunt."

The saddest thing of all isn't the beating I've just taken, but the lie I'll have to tell my parents. I can never tell them, or anyone else, about the damage Geoff is inflicting upon me.

I sneak into the house late at night, avoiding my parents, because there's no way I can tell a lie without cracking. I retreat to my bedroom and look at myself in the full-length mirror. I can't see anything objectively. The insults have taken a toll. I'm no longer the cute girl that boys want to date, girls want to befriend, but a hideous monster made of angles and bones. I spit at my reflection.

If my parents catch a whiff of my self-loathing, they'll lose their minds. They've always loved and encouraged me, but Geoff has me convinced that I'm revolting and delusional.

Take the day I was crowned Homecoming Queen, for instance. Amid the excitement and hoopla, Geoff let me know that my popularity and success were figments of my grandiose imagination. After the dance, we got in the car to drive around and bleed off some of the afternoon's energy, and he said, just as we pulled out of the student parking lot, "Take off that crown, idiot. Just who do you think you are?" Instead of acting hurt, I apologized and took off the sparkling tiara, tucked it beneath the skirt of my dress.

Nothing I do satisfies Geoff. I'm disorganized. I don't like the right foods, don't have the right friends. He hates the way I drive, yet insists on me driving so he can grab the wheel and tell me I'm stupid. "You don't know what you're doing. This is ridiculous. Pull over." When we ordered fish from a takeout restaurant, he said, "Get extra lemon." I scurried back with so many lemon wedges, a whole lemon, but it wasn't enough. Then he cursed me out and called me names for getting it all wrong. He does this stuff all the time.

I grab Louise, my cat, and sit on my bed. I recount to her every nasty name Geoff calls me; I describe every smack, kick, and spit. Louise, all ten pounds of her, is my rock. She lets me cry into her soft gray fur for hours while I hold her. Her purrs soothe me. It's as though she's telling me it will all be okay. She knows every horrible secret I keep and there's nobody else I can tell.

The next morning, even before I enter the kitchen, where I can hear my parents talking, I come up with a story to explain the obvious damage to my face, the swelling, the double black eyes: because of my jealousy over Geoff, I got into a fight with another girl. I'm a horrible liar, but I have no other choice. Geoff has threatened to break up with me if my parents ever find out. There's no escaping the demand for some plausible explanation.

My parents nearly go nuts at the sight of me standing there by the stove, swollen almost beyond recognition. They can't imagine that I would ever sit still for a beating, so they believe the lie. They can't imagine such a troubled, violent relationship. When we kids fought at the dining room table, our parents wouldn't let us leave the table until we'd worked it out, which we always did.

"Knock off the jealousy stuff!" my mother says, on the verge of tears. We used to have family dinners every single night when I was young, but if my dad wasn't home by six o'clock, if he was running late, Mom would feed us kids and sit with us, then eat with Dad when he got home. She never picked up her fork until my dad got home, that's how much she loved and respected him. It's not that he expected such devotion; it's what she wanted to do. Jealousy isn't part of her vocabulary, nor is it in Dad's. Their language is all about mutual respect.

Two things happen after I tell this lie. First, because of the need for deception in order to be with Geoff, I grow more distant from the people who mean the world to me, particularly my watchful parents. And second, Geoff convinces me that the beatings are my fault. If only I were smarter or prettier, gained some weight, or were how he wants me to be, he wouldn't have to punish me.

First the abuser isolates you; then the abuser makes you question yourself.

{ 4 }

HIGH HEELS IN
THE LAUNDRY ROOM

I PULLED MY CAR over, banged my head against the steering wheel, and screamed at the top of my lungs, "I HATE BOSTON!" I was blind with frustration that I was lost, yet again. I gave the finger out the window to nobody in particular—just to the city. A nun or a little old lady could have passed by at that moment, but I wouldn't have seen them or cared. I hated Boston because it gave a whole new meaning to the word *lost*.

I was only a few months into my new career, and I felt like quitting every day. What the hell was I thinking, putting myself out there as a delivery service? It was clear that I wasn't thinking. Most of the time, I had no idea what I was doing.

I had no sense of direction. I'd get a job and end up going around and around in circles for what felt like hours, finally locating the pickup point in some inconspicuous strip mall. Once there, I'd lug boxes that weighed more than I did, shove them in my car, make the deliveries—up and down flights of stairs, to loading docks, basements—every muscle shaking under the weight. The streets of Boston, however, made everything one hundred times worse. Half the street signs were missing, or placed in a spot no one would think to look, at least me; the other half were one-way streets that dropped me four blocks farther than I intended to go. Around and around the maze I would go.

There was no calling my dispatchers when I was off track. First, I didn't have dispatchers, let alone help of any kind. Second, there was no such thing as cell phones at that time. I would forward customer calls from the phone I'd had installed in my mother's laundry room to my pager.

In case you don't remember, a pager was a little square box that displayed the telephone number of the person trying to reach you. Drug dealers clipped them on their belts to let them know when a customer was calling in search of a fix. Doctors wore them whenever they were on call (probably some still do), so they could race to the hospital. Whenever my pager would go off, I'd have to stop what I was doing and find a pay phone to return my customer's call. Do you remember pay phones? They used to be on busy street corners for public use. Usually, the booths were covered in graffiti and filled with condom wrappers. Half the time the receiver had been ripped off the thick silver phone cord. Of course, I wouldn't have any money for the pay phone, so I'd have to scrounge for change—digging at the bottom of my purse, between the car seat cushions, in the glove compartment. Or I could use the single credit card I owned, the one the phone company had given me to make calls after they'd installed my line and verified I had (very little) cash in my bank account. Apparently, $150 was enough to satisfy Ma Bell.

I was a disaster, but that's how I started. Making calls, delivering packages, with calls forwarded to my pager. A fifteen-dollar job here, a ten-dollar job there. I was on my way, even though it didn't feel like it then.

In those very early days, I lived in the red. I'd do a delivery one day, then call my customer the next day, asking them to pay me because I had no money, begging them not to wait the usual thirty days to settle the bill. I'd drive to their office so they could hand me a check. From there, I'd scurry to the bank, deposit the check, then pay myself so I could get gas and do the next delivery. I'd write checks to cover my expenses, then beg customers to pay me so I could cover them before they bounced. I also had to make car payments to Geoff. I pictured being picked up for check fraud and going straight to jail—that's how close I was to the cliff's edge.

Most of the time, my customers would comply because I was young and earnest and they felt bad for me. They could see I was a hustler, like them, that I had drive, so they admired that. But they could also sense that I was nervous and barely making ends meet, so they wanted to rescue me. Plus, I was too naive to know that you should never tell a customer that you need money so you can buy gas for your car because it makes you sound desperate, and desperation stinks.

Not long after I started, I realized that delivering little jobs wasn't going to cut it. I needed to get to the next level.

"I need more," I told my mom over the kitchen table after I'd spent the entire day chasing my tail for peanuts. "I can't keep doing these ten-dollar jobs. I need more."

Talk about having an angel looking out for you.

In addition to using my Rolodex and the Yellow Pages, I literally knocked on doors to drum up business. Out on my door-knocking rounds the next day, I walked into Output Technologies (OTI), Inc. Usually, there was a young woman behind the desk sorting files and answering phones. She would chat with me for a minute or two while I told her why I was there, then point to the ubiquitous sign hung in the lobby that read No Soliciting, a polite way of indicating that I should leave. But that day, the operations director happened to be walking past and, having heard what I was pitching, said, "Why don't you come in." Taking a seat behind his desk, he said that it was good timing because they'd just fired their courier company. I reached into my briefcase to pull out my rate sheet when he asked, "Are you 24/7 ?" He was asking if I had the capacity to deliver twenty-four hours a day, seven days a week, which actually meant I was about to negotiate away my social life, as if I had one to begin with, and the ability to sleep. I'd distanced myself from friends in favor of spending time with Geoff; I'd spent months on Gina's couch licking my wounds after he'd dumped me; now I worked nonstop, which made hanging out with Shea and Juls, the only two friends who continued to stick by me, next to impossible.

"Absolutely, I'm 24/7," I said, without a moment of hesitation. "I've got twenty drivers. A fleet of trucks. I can definitely handle your work." I sat there with a can-do grin plastered on my face, eyes wide open, my demeanor perky, but inside I was screaming. *Oh my God, I've got nobody. I've got myself! Me, my pager, and my prestigious office in my parents' laundry room.*

I walked out of OTI and did what any top-level executive would do: I called my mom at the nearest pay phone. "Mom, I just landed the biggest customer!" I hopped up and down as the cars whizzed past. The wind was blowing, sending my hair swirling around me. I didn't know how I was going to handle the job; how was I supposed to work day and night shifts? I just knew I'd do whatever I had to do, that I'd move heaven and earth to get it done. I'd figure it out as I went along. I'd build the plane as I flew it. For the first time, I wasn't thinking about proving Geoff wrong. I could see how the thing might come together, and that thrilled me.

Sure enough, OTI needed somebody 24/7. I had to hire a part-time driver for the night shift.

I placed a twenty-dollar ad in the *Patriot Ledger*, and three days later there was Eddie. He was friendly, easygoing, passive even; a year or two older than me, and still living at home with his mother. From the smell of things, he spent his days smoking pot in the basement. But he was willing to work as a team, knowing that neither of us had a clue as to what we were really supposed to do. He knew that I was learning the ropes, that I had just about as much experience as he had, which was next to none, and that I was willing to take his suggestions into account when we divvied up the day. We agreed that I'd do the deliveries until one o'clock in the morning, then turn the jobs over to him until seven o'clock.

Just as my head hit the pillow, OTI paged me with a delivery. I called Eddie. "Okay, we have a pickup at OTI, going over to State Street. Can you cover it?" Picturing him falling asleep the moment we hung up, because God knows how much pot he'd been smoking, I said, "You're up, right? You're up?"

"Yeah, I'm up."

"Let me hear your feet touch the floor. Put the phone on the floor and let me hear your feet."

"Michelle, I'm up, I'm up."

But I insisted because I knew what could happen when you're bone tired, even if you're a good person and you mean well and you haven't finished off a dime bag an hour before. "No, no, no. Put the phone on the floor. Let me hear your feet touch the floor."

And he did it. I could hear his feet touch the floor.

"Okay. Call me when you pick it up. Then call me when you deliver it." I would have done the delivery myself, taken Eddie out of the equation altogether, but even I knew one sleepless night after another would be unsustainable. As long as I micromanaged Eddie, and he accepted that as part of the job, I could slowly learn to trust him to protect my fledgling company.

This scenario played out night after night. I had to trust that Eddie would get the job done, but there was no room to screw up. You are only as good as your last delivery. One wrong move in this unforgiving business and I'd be back on the street making endless cold calls in industrial parks for penny-ante jobs, eating ramen at ten o'clock at night, and driving around on gas fumes. I wasn't going to lose my big chance. I wasn't going to let the competition swoop in and steal my clients just because I'd failed to meet one deadline, shown the slightest sign of unreliability. I was building my business off such mistakes.

"All right, all right..." he said. And that became the story of my life for a good long time.

OTI kept me ridiculously busy. On top of that, I was still making cold calls for new customers every day; there was no way to avoid that if I wanted to grow. Soon I was working around the clock. Whenever I went out to dinner with my family, I'd have to leave to do a delivery. They'd watch me get up from the table, a mix of disappointment and concern playing across their faces, and tell me to go on. In the car, I'd feel so sorry for myself, I'd cry and cry.

I hated the job, and I loved it. To anyone who would listen, I'd say, "I have no life!" and "I don't know how this is going to work. I have nothing. All I'm doing is working." But I loved the job because it was mine. I was making it. I had traction in my business. I was forming great business relationships. People trusted me. They liked me, respected me. It just seemed to come at such an incredible cost. Before, I'd given over my identity to Geoff; now, I was giving it over to my job. Michelle did not exist.

Meanwhile, my friends were going out and having fun, but I just didn't have time to join them.

"Come on, Michelle. Sell that stupid company," Shea and Juls said while getting ready for a night of clubbing, doing up their makeup and teasing their hair, while I sat on Gina's couch in pajamas and slippers, knowing I had early morning deliveries. I knew they'd have fun, toss back some drinks, dance with some cute guys, and come back at two in the morning, laughing too loud. The truth was, I felt alone, and in some ways I missed Geoff.

One week, the girls packed for a cruise, adding one more cute sundress here, one more pair of strappy sandals there to their already overflowing suitcases stationed in the middle of the living room. Day after day, they begged me to join them in the Caribbean, to take some much-deserved time off. I refused. The only thing I was packing was a carful of boxes to be delivered in sloppy, ten-degree weather. Standing in my snow boots and parka, I told myself, "It's okay. It's going to be good." Yet I wasn't sure. What was I trying to prove?

I was bent over my parents' kitchen table, crying my eyes out the day after my friends left without me. "This sucks," I told my mother. "I have no life. I hate this! I'm selling this stupid business!"

I felt my dad tapping me on the shoulder. "Mish, is it really worth anything?"

I wasn't sure what he was asking. Was my business worth anything to a buyer? Was the toll extracted from me worth the payoff? "No. Yes. I don't know! I have no life…"

Then my dad said, "Get your head up, wipe those tears, blow your nose, and knock it off. If anyone can do it, you can." My dad had quit school at a very young age to help provide for his family. His father had gone out for a loaf of bread one evening and never come home, leaving his mother to raise three young children alone. It was a hard life for my grandmother, and I'm sure there were rough times for my dad, not having a father in his life. If anyone understood that a person had to do what needed to be done no matter how they felt, it was Dad.

I did what my dad commanded, and I got on with my life. I just plugged along. I stayed at it because giving up wasn't an option.

I went to work in the laundry room every day from that day forward dressed in a suit and heels. I'd walk past the kitchen on the way to my "office" and my dad would hear the *click click click*.

He'd say, "Mish, where are you going today dressed like that? You're only going to the laundry room."

I'd reply, "No, Dad, I'm going to *work*." The woman I envisioned becoming was professional, beautiful, and powerful. Like it or not, heels command respect. You want success, you dress for it first. You play the part, and reality follows accordingly.

I wanted my business to succeed, so I pushed myself hard. I was consumed with every single detail—potential opportunities and possible pitfalls—but there was something else at play. I found strength I didn't know I had. I found myself more able to resist Geoff.

Each time I landed a new account, I found myself talking to an imaginary Geoff. "I just landed that account. I *am* a smart person! See!"

Sometimes I forgot to tell him, and I'd just tell myself: *See, Michelle, you are smart*.

I treated work as not just another escape, but a form of therapy. I put myself wholeheartedly into it—completely, 100 percent. I challenged myself in so many ways. Most of what I did, I hadn't realized I was capable of doing. I was desperate and figured I had nothing to lose, even if I never won Geoff back. It was live or die, my choice. So I chose to live.

I was heading in a healthier direction, but I still lacked confidence. Business success aside, I was still unsure and insecure. I heard myself saying, "I'm sorry," a thousand times a day. Every other word out of my mouth was some form of apology. "I'm sorry I didn't catch your call." "I'm sorry, where is the bathroom?" "I'm sorry to be in the wrong parking spot." Despite the heels and suit I wore to the laundry room every day, I had trouble seeing myself as an attractive girl. When I looked in the mirror, I saw a ninety-pound, bloodshot-eyed worker bee.

I was still seeing my therapist every week. She'd say, "Michelle, try to have a positive thought about yourself today.

Try to do something good for yourself." She made me feel I was someone worthy of care.

When I had the money, I started to buy some nice clothes, get my eyebrows waxed, go outside and meet people. I surrounded myself with family and friends who were positive and nourishing for me. I started to exercise and eat well. I even put on some weight.

Without being aware of it, as I was building my business, I was also rebuilding myself.

Build the plane while you fly it.

{ 5 }

QUICKSAND

GEOFF BUYS THE diamond ring off a friend whose engagement went awry. That should be a sign, but of course I'm long past paying attention to signs.

As I stand on the Legacy loading dock, where we've been waiting to unload a truck, Geoff looking up at me on bended knee, ring in hand, I experience waves of conflicting emotions. At first blush I'm excited, even overjoyed. I make a show of pulling him to his feet, hugging him as hard as I can, bouncing up and down. But inside, a part of me is screaming, *What the hell are you doing? This guy is so bad for you. You're going to wind up dead.*

I accept the proposal and the ring without hesitation, but instead of slipping the diamond on my finger, I shove it in my pocket. More than anything, I'm terrified to tell my parents. They'll be mortified by the turn of events.

My parents hate Geoff. After graduating from high school, I chose not to go to college because I didn't want to leave Geoff behind. They blamed him for my decision to take the year off and figure myself out because he begged me to stay behind with him. I didn't really know what I wanted to do anyway, but they aren't inclined to take that into account. Geoff had just opened a dry cleaner's and asked me to help out, so I did. I also took a job waitressing in a Mexican restaurant so the two of us could have some extra cash, because neither of us was flush. When I turned twenty, Geoff decided to start Legacy Signs and asked me to help with that as well. According to him, he had the finances and I had the time.

Considering our history, the constant breakups, his serial cheating, I didn't think we should work together at Legacy; too much time together would further strain our relationship. I told him so, but he convinced me it would be fine. "No, it's going to work out. We're gonna be great working together."

Geoff was forever breaking up with me, which is another reason my parents hate his guts. We've been off and on, off and on, more times than I can list here. He'd be with me for six months, and then cheat on me and break up with me, leaving me an absolute mess. It would take everybody to pick me up and help me through the trauma. They took sweet care of me, only to see me fall into the cycle all over again. Everybody knew I was completely obsessed with Geoff and deaf to reason. If I depended on him now for my livelihood, I'd be even more vulnerable.

Sick of witnessing my pain, my parents forbade me to see Geoff whenever we broke up, and I swore, each and every time, I'd never see him again. Time and time again, he'd call me because it didn't work out with whomever he was with, and I'd fly right back into his arms. Just when I'd started to get over him, he'd ask me back and I'd go, like a lamb to the slaughter. This was the predictable pattern I considered before placing all my eggs in the Legacy basket, while fingering the engagement ring in my pocket.

My father cottoned on to the fact that I was sneaking around to see Geoff again, which is how it always went. Dad and I got into a battle right in the middle of the living room one night, and Dad stormed out after Geoff. "Never see my daughter again," he screamed the moment he next caught sight of Geoff, at the dry cleaner's. "You think you can treat her like garbage, you've got another think coming. You'll have me to deal with."

I begged my dad, "Dad, just let me be with him."

Geoff and I played out this drama hundreds of times, each time breaking my parents' hearts. They'd go to bed and pray that someday I'd be free of him, but I never was.

Geoff always acts like I'm a crazy, jealous bitch, and that's why he was forced to end our relationship all those times. I question my perception, my entire grip on reality. Maybe I see things that aren't there. Maybe I falsely accuse Geoff of sins he'd never commit. Sure, he flirts with girls, but he never means anything by it. He was so insulted by my reaction the night at the stoplight that he beat me nearly senseless. When will I ever learn to keep my fears and doubts to my stupid self?

There was, however, a girl who lived across from the dry cleaner's whom I just knew he'd hooked up with. He denied my accusations, but I could tell by the way they looked at each other. Whenever she came into the dry cleaner's, she'd say, "I'm here to pick up my dry cleaning," and they'd share this look. I knew the truth deep in my bones. But he'd always turn it around, so I never knew what was white or black or up or down.

I forever wonder who in the crowd he's slept with, who in the crowd he's trying to pick up. I'm always being played for a fool, made to think I'm stark raving mad. And I am.

Like an alcoholic depends on a drink, like a drug addict depends on a drug, I need Geoff to function. I'm so dependent on him that I can't imagine my life without him. The thought of not having him at the center of my world is worse than feeling played or abused by him. I get my high from being with him. Then he leaves and the high wears off. I'm left feeling empty, cold, and numb. At the first opportunity, I'll race right back for another hit. I know myself.

He can beat, slap, insult, and chastise me, but as long as I get my fix, I can function.

I don't care that my parents and friends hate him, that everyone knows he cheats on me. When people say I'm crazy for dating him, I don't care. I just want him. I can never walk away from Geoff; I don't know how.

Since we started the sign business together, we work ninety hours a week. I still live at my parents' house, and I don't spend more than ten hours a week there. I'm lucky if I sleep there a whole night; most nights I work and sleep on the manufacturing floor. So it makes perfect sense that he asks me to marry him on a loading dock while waiting to unload a truck.

I pull the ring out of my pocket after working up the courage and show it to my parents, tell them we're engaged. My parents go pale. Their jaws hang slack. With so little choice in the matter, and after all they've been through with me, they know they have no choice. Eventually, they feign acceptance. I sport the ring on my finger and start to make wedding plans.

Shortly thereafter, Geoff and I move in together, against my parents' wishes. They feel very strongly against their kids moving in with someone before we're married, least of all a man who's put me through the wringer. But my mom, being as wonderful as she is, buys me a ton of stuff for the apartment, including some nice bowls. I think, *This is great, this is going to work. We're going to get married.*

I'm twenty-two and I assume that a few bowls and a ring will make me the lady of the house.

Your gut knows, even when you choose to ignore it.

———————————

{ 6 }

HELP COMES
AT DIFFERENT COSTS

Y MOTHER SAT with me at the kitchen table one Friday evening, looking over my books while I ate the supper she'd prepared for me. "Michelle," she said, "you're in the red. You just paid your two drivers and their checks are going to bounce."

Mom didn't really need to look at the numbers to know how close to the edge I was playing it. She worked next door to the post office and would run over to my PO box each day to see if any payments had come in. (I'd shelled out for a PO box as it was more professional than using my parents' home address.) She'd call me while she opened the checks, reading off the amounts one at a time. I'd cross my fingers, plug the numbers into my calculator, praying they'd add up to the figure I needed to cover the two part-time drivers I now needed to handle the growing business. It was like playing the lottery, hoping the right combination of numbers came up and paid off. I'm sure Mom felt as though she was playing the lottery right along with me.

I held my breath when I paid the drivers each Friday afternoon, hoping that on Monday I'd receive more checks so I could deposit them in time to prevent the bounce. For the most part I was successful, but there were times when those checks were pure rubber. I'd be so embarrassed, having promised the drivers that the checks were good to clear. They forgave me, because they knew I was naive and had no idea how to run a business. They cut me slack because they felt sorry for me. They also saw how hard I was trying. I was out there doing deliveries, answering phones, trying to sell, and doing the books. Even so, I knew it was only a matter of time before their patience ran out.

I didn't have to tell my mother I was out there doing everything I could possibly do to bring in money; she saw that was the case. She also understood what it was to live paycheck to paycheck. Despite the occasional setback, my parents did what they could to provide a great home for us. Mom and Dad had given their kids everything they could, even if it meant they had to go without. For Mom that meant sometimes she had to drive around in a car with a door held on by a rope. Making a living wasn't always easy; making the money stretch could sometimes feel impossible. Mom appreciated that struggle.

To make accounting matters worse, neither my mother nor I understood a thing about paying corporate or employment taxes. Sure, we'd both filled out personal income tax statements and mailed them to the IRS before April 15, but we hadn't a clue that I needed to file a federal deposit every month, to report taxes. To whom? When? Where? How the heck was I supposed to know any of that? Believe me when I tell you that the government was far less forgiving than my drivers. You don't get brownie points for ignorance, or for trying really hard. "You're doing great, honey," my mother said, even though we both knew she was lying.

Before long, I picked up a couple of regular customers, one being Keystone Inks. Keystone Inks was a family-owned company that operated out of their house in Norwood. Nathan and Helene were the owners. They knew that I was a small company—well, that my company consisted of me and maybe one or two drivers, depending on volume, and my part-time assistant, Auntie Katie.

Katie had begun taking orders for me the day my younger brother got into a terrible car accident, and I couldn't hope to focus on business. My family had gone into emergency overdrive like they always did when one of us was in trouble. There was no alternative as far as I was concerned, business or no. Not knowing where else to turn, I called my auntie in a panic and asked her to come over and answer my phone. Once my brother was out of danger, I returned to the office and found that I loved having Katie around. Now, while I was out selling in my high heels and short skirts, Katie was at the bumper pool table multitasking away. None of the customers on the other end of the line had a clue that she was breastfeeding and sitting in a laundry room navigating the noisy spin cycle while a clueless twenty-three-year-old made all the executive decisions.

Keystone Inks kept me busy. I'd deliver a package, then call Nathan the very next day and ask him to pay me. He'd say, "Oh, Michelle, am I past due?" I'd say, "No, Nathan, I just did the job yesterday." Then they'd pay me, just as I asked. Their business gave me just enough cash to quell the panic.

The Supersonic Ink Company, owned by Ed and Betty, was my second new, promising conquest—possibly bigger than Keystone Inks. They used a different courier company at the time but decided to give me a shot, for which I was exceedingly grateful. I knew them from the sign manufacturing days, although not that well, and I assumed that's what allowed me to get my foot in the door. I didn't care about the loose connection to Geoff because it meant more money to pay my drivers.

After I did a number of local deliveries for Supersonic, popping in and out of their office on a regular basis, Betty asked me if I knew of anyone who could answer their phones. They knew I had my finger on the pulse of a number of businesses in the area and would likely spot a receptionist on the way out, or know of someone networking for a job. My sister happened to be out of work at the time, so, shortly after I made the connection, they hired her part-time. She worked for them for a few months before she ended up getting a full-time job, leaving them once again without help answering their phones.

Again, Betty approached me for help. This time she asked if I wanted to operate out of their office, if I wanted to work out a win-win arrangement.

"What, move my business out of the laundry room into your office?" I asked. I'd made a joke early on, letting them know I was just starting out, working like a maniac out of my parents' house, which was all I could afford. I'd discovered that nice people are usually willing to champion the underdog.

"You can forward your phones to one of our lines and use a desk and pay no rent," she said. "In return, you can answer our phones."

It was getting lonely sitting in the laundry room working all hours of the day and night. When I was there, Katie wasn't, and of course both my parents were off at work until nearly six o'clock, which left huge stretches of the day for me to listen to nothing but the sound of my own heart, which was usually racing a mile a minute, or the rustle of phone book pages. In between admin tasks and paperwork, I'd talk to customers, prospects, or one of the drivers, but I still felt all alone. At this time I only had a job here and there; I wasn't always out making deliveries, but spent more time trying to gather clients for the business. It was bad enough that I couldn't go out with my friends and I wasn't dating anyone and my office was in a laundry room. Aside from my parents, plus Shea and Gina at their apartment, I had little communication with the outside world unless it involved delivering packages. So I took Betty up on their offer.

I packed up some boxes and moved out of the laundry room over the weekend. I call-forwarded my phone to one of Supersonic's lines and set up shop at one of their desks. At this point Katie had left to take another job with benefits, so I was in charge of my own line as well as all of Supersonic's. I placed my calculator in one corner, my Rolodex in the other, and dropped an extra pair of shoes and a spare set of pantyhose in the bottom drawer. Monday morning, I got off the couch and drove to a real office. Okay, it wasn't *mine*, but it was a nice feeling. I settled in and started to answer my phone along with theirs. Things ran smoothly, and I got to enjoy the sights and sounds of people hustling around me, moving from office to office, slugging back tea.

We started to form a nice relationship, going out to dinner from time to time. Ed and Betty were really good to me, and it felt wonderful to be working away building my business while helping them with theirs. I'd gotten used to people helping me when I could do little to pay them back. I much preferred this arrangement.

Little by little, the dynamic shifted. It dawned on me one morning that I was doing more work for them than for myself. I was on their phone taking orders for them when my line rang. I had a separate line that I couldn't answer if I was running their phones. One ring, two rings, three rings, four. Nobody answered. The number appeared on my pager. Sometimes customers would call vendor two if they didn't connect with another person on the line, or if they didn't receive a call back right away. Then it happened again, an hour later, then again. It went on like that for the day, then several days in a row. When they went away on vacation for a week, I ran their company as well as mine. They were so sure that their business was being handled that they never once called in to check. Having no understanding of boundaries, I had no idea what was my responsibility and what was theirs.

To make matters worse, I doubted my perceptions. These were lovely people who only wanted to see me succeed; I had to be reading it wrong. So exhausted was I from my uncertainty, I decided I would pay closer attention, just to be sure I wasn't overreacting. Sure enough, whenever their phone rang, Ed would pick up the other line and pretend to be busy with a customer. I looked around and Betty couldn't be found, which meant I was compelled to answer. The minute my phone rang, Ed would race to the file cabinet or speak into a dead phone, so he wouldn't have to cover mine. I envisioned losing hundreds of dollars with each missed call, which made me break into a cold sweat, and I wondered what I'd gotten myself into. Later I would learn that abusive situations never get better—they only get worse. I'd learned this lesson with Geoff, seen how that stuff starts then escalates, but there I was learning the very same lesson again.

I went to my parents' house and described what was going on. My father and mother listened intently, asked me a few questions, then gave each other a knowing look. That look confirmed that I was not paranoid. Mom said, "Michelle, you need to come back to the house and get back to your business." Coming from Mom, who'd been regularly caught in her bathrobe making breakfast for my dad as drivers traipsed in and out, the worst one being a Charles Manson lookalike whom I'd interviewed but never hired, this statement meant a lot.

The following weekend, when nobody from Supersonic was around, I packed up my stuff in yet another cardboard box and headed back to the laundry room. Home sweet home. I even turned on the dryer for the familiar thrum.

I heard from Ed and Betty only once, when I received a two-page letter from them saying that all they'd done was help me and I'd repaid them by walking out on them in their time of need. They included a check for some outstanding delivery invoices and that was that. The letter made me feel guilty and angry all at the same time. I was grateful for the payment, although I'd written it off in my head, chalking it up to a number of relatively cheap lessons.

Years later, one of my drivers was out doing a delivery and ran into Ed at a local coffee shop. Ed saw the Xpressman lettering on his truck. "Is that Michelle Cully's company you work for?" Ed asked.

"Yes," my driver responded.

"Oh, I helped her start that company."

If I had a nickel for every time someone tried to take credit for my company, I wouldn't have had to work so hard, because I'd be rich.

Half the battle is learning to trust your instincts.

{ 7 }

BROKE AND DUMB

OUR WEDDING IS scheduled for October 23. Instead of feeling excited, with each day I check off on the calendar, I feel more and more that I'm facing a death sentence. Things have only gotten worse now that we share a roof.

Everything I do or say, no matter how innocuous, is fodder for an argument.

Geoff claims he doesn't trust me, even though I've never done anything to warrant mistrust. He watches everything I do, listens to every conversation, and won't let me out of his sight. By choice, I'm with him practically 24/7, but that still doesn't fix our problems.

I've come to think of Geoff's jealousy as an expression of love. In a twisted way, I love that he's jealous. I love that he doesn't want me to dress up or to let me out of his sight. It makes me feel important. I think it shows he cares, even though it's a constant source of discord.

Everything you can imagine, Geoff controls. Everything. The money, the apartment where we live, the car I drive, the job I have, the friends I talk to or don't talk to, what I wear.

Despite the ridiculous workweeks I put in, I receive an allowance of $10 per day, which he thinks fair because he pays the rent and the car bills. If I want to buy something, he has to approve it, or I have to hide it from him to avoid a knock-down, drag-out fight. If I want to buy pretty clothes to spruce up my game after he's accused me of being a slob, I charge them to my credit card and hope he won't see. When I shop, I hit the deep-discount department stores so he'll have little reason to complain.

I buy a bikini on the sly one day, then dare to put it on and model it for him, to impress him. Geoff rips it off my body and shreds it to pieces. To show me who's boss, to keep that concept front and center, he snaps my lipsticks in half so I can't use them, breaks the heels off my stilettos. I buy a pair of replacement shoes for $15 and hide them from him for a couple of weeks. I pull them out and leave them around our apartment, so he'll get used to seeing them around. When he notices them and questions me, I say my sister bought them for me.

I'm afraid to go down the street and get a slice of pizza for $2. "Geoff, can I please have $2 to get a slice of pizza?" "Can I have $10 to put some gas in my car?"

The money dynamic was set up right from the beginning. Geoff's uncle loaned him the money we needed to rent an empty warehouse for Legacy. Then Geoff got a small business loan and bought a couple of pieces of equipment. According to him, all I do is sit in the office answering phones, manage the accounts payable and accounts receivable, and take orders. We both know that I really don't know what I'm doing. Truly, I just wing it, so I figure maybe he's right. Maybe, if we're going to get ahead, he needs to manage all of the finances.

For the first five months, it was just us running Legacy, then Geoff started recruiting others, giving jobs to each of his family members and a handful of friends. It's the only sign manufacturer in that area, so it's a real gold mine. We work endless hours, fall asleep on the manufacturing floor, then get up and work some more. I go out and pick us up lunch, then we eat and get right back to work.

Say what you will about my lack of experience, Geoff and I have built a business with our hearts and souls. We've put every ounce of ourselves into it. "This is ours," Geoff says as we lie there on the dusty cement. "This is for our family. This is going to be our life for our children." In those moments, he almost makes me believe he considers me an equal partner, despite the endless criticisms and death grip on the purse strings, and despite the fact that it's always been just his name on the title.

My intelligence, or lack thereof, is another source of criticism from Geoff, as well as from his family. I'm not just ugly and skinny, but stupid too.

I overhear his mom and younger sister trash-talking me one day. "You know, she's not the brightest star in the sky," one of them says. "She's not the brightest bulb in the box."

When I cry because my darkest fears have been validated, Geoff simply says, "Well, what do you expect?"

Geoff magnifies that insecurity a hundredfold, but it's been there all along, the crack that let him enter in the first place.

From the beginning, school was difficult for me. I never felt smart enough. When I was in kindergarten, I went to a Catholic school. One of the nuns slapped my hand with a ruler in front of the whole class because I couldn't spell "hockey puck." She made me cry—not from the slap, but from the embarrassment. She intentionally made a fool out of me, asking me over and over again how to spell the word. Every time I tried, it was wrong, and she would make me spell it again.

When I told him what had happened, my dad got up from the dinner table and called the school. While he screamed at the nun, I sat there, gloating over my rigatoni and sauce. I felt vindicated and loved by my dad, the way he stood up for me. That's what people who love you do: they defend you, no matter who they have to cross.

I always thought of my peers as smarter than me. I had to get "extra help" in school. Back then, everyone called it the "special room" or the "stupid room," the place I had to go for reading and comprehension. I found the whole exercise so embarrassing that I'd sneak into the room each day so nobody would see me. That special room was just for us "dummies."

So when Geoff starts in with the "stupid" and "idiot" comments, it strikes a chord. It never occurs to Geoff to take umbrage with his mother and sister for trash-talking me. Maybe I am too dumb to defend.

Now that we live together and are making preparations to marry, I know that I've painted myself into a corner. I realize that not only am I stupid, I no longer have an identity or free will.

Before Geoff, I was so happy, and was even voted "happiest" in seventh grade. I loved hanging with my friends, loved being with my family. I loved to shop for clothes, yet I would give the shirt off my back to someone who needed it. I always cried if someone else was sad. I just wanted to be happy, and for everyone else to be happy too.

I am a girl, not even a woman, who's lost herself. I've lost my belief in myself. I'm stupid and ugly, not only physically but inside. I've been stripped of myself.

There's plenty of information available about domestic abuse; it's always in my face. It's in the news every other week. My mother once said, "Why would someone stay in that situation?" I have a pain inside me, and I think, *I know why they do it, I know why they stay.*

Someone can insult your intelligence and criticize your lack of education. What they can't do is steal your integrity.

———————————

{ 8 }

GUARD DOGS
AND TRUCKS

I LOOKED OUT THE window with a huge smile, staring at row upon row of gray headstones surrounded by a chain-link fence. I couldn't believe I had a *real* office, even if it was only one room overlooking the dead. It was *mine*: Xpressman Trucking and Courier, Inc. My company name was even on a little wooden plaque in the lobby. Around the six-month mark, my parents had finally given me the boot, due to the increased traffic through their kitchen, the incessant stream of motley characters who did deliveries for me from time to time. Terrified I wouldn't be able to afford the rent—$100 per month including utilities—I knew I would have to pull it off or die trying. How ironic that would be, to wind up six feet under, right across the street from my expensive office.

I turned my attention back to my mom, who sat on the opposite side of my desk, a stack of papers between us. I'd hired her, as well as her friend Paula, to help me run the office since Katie had landed another managerial position. Mom studied each driver's manifest, which was a log sheet of all the jobs the driver had done. Riffling through the paper pile, she found the sheet where I logged all of the deliveries. She ran a finger down the list until she found the name she was looking for, then made a cost notation in a separate document. When she was done matching the driver to the job, she added up the figures on her calculator. God bless Mom. She would stay with me until ten or eleven o'clock Thursday nights figuring out how much to bill the customer and how much to pay the individual driver. Together, we would look at the mileage, review the price of the job, and double-check the driver percentage, not just for one driver but for however many we had at any given moment. Mom wouldn't leave until we balanced everything. It was awful work, yet my mother, who'd quit her job making cotton candy so she could help me out, never complained. Nor did she expect payment for her labor because she knew I could barely afford to pay myself, or cover the new rent.

Tired of the mind-numbing number crunching, I stared out the opposite window, just beyond my mother's head. From this vantage point, I could see directly into Metro Courier's parking lot. My competitor's fleet of trucks pulled in and out of their gate. I said to Mom, who had found another mistake to attack with her eraser, "One day we'll have that. We'll have a fleet of trucks. It may take a while, but I promise we will."

"If anyone can make that happen, honey, it's you."

I took a bite of the sandwich my mother had made for me before coming to work. I chewed thoughtfully. First step first: I needed to lease a truck.

"COME ON, SEAN. Let's see if this place rents trucks."

I was driving around Brockton with a new full-time truck driver. I'd started to make a little money and decided the time was right to rent my own truck.

"You stay here, I'll go in." I hopped out of my car and took in the truck rental parking lot. It was after five o'clock and I wasn't sure if anyone was still there. I spotted what appeared to be an office, just beyond a construction trailer and a filthy Bobcat. I proceeded to tiptoe through the muddy lot in my short white skirt and matching jacket, which looked more like a lab coat than a blazer, white hose, and badass orange high heels. I hadn't gone two steps before the backs of my legs were splattered with muck.

"Hello? Anyone here?" I heard nothing beyond the whizz of traffic past the security fence, the sloshing of my feet.

I scanned the lot and then I heard something else: a long, low growl. I froze mid-step. Slowly looking down, I spotted the source of the ominous noise. With his not-so-pearly whites bared and drool dripping from his lips, the hound from hell growled again. A collared German shepherd on an indeterminate length of chain—not good.

"Nice doggie," I said in my fake calm voice, the very same one I'd used with Geoff when I could sense his anger. Little by little, as inconspicuously as I could manage in light of being scared out of my wits, I turned away. I took some quick baby steps toward my car, praying to Mother Mary that I might remain in one piece, with a normal volume of blood coursing through my veins. That's when the animal leaped.

"Sean!" I screamed as I tore across the parking lot, mud now drenching the hem of my skirt, the collar of my jacket. Cujo was in hot pursuit; I could hear his paws slapping behind me as he picked up speed. My heart pounded.

Jesus Christ! How long is that chain? I turned around to check. Then, before I knew what was happening, the animal lunged and bit me square in the ass. I screamed again. "Sean!" And then, bam, the dog jumped up and bit my ass again. Still running, I turned again. This time, the creature had finally reached the end of his chain. One more forward bound and the dog jerked off his feet and slammed onto his back. I slid into my car as if it were home plate, the last game of the World Series.

Catching my breath, I looked around to confirm that I was safe. Sean stood just beyond the open passenger door, clutching his sides, laughing so hard he couldn't take a breath. It took me a moment to connect with what he was doing, laughing at my near-death experience. I put my head down and laughed until I cried. I couldn't stop. The release felt so good. I hadn't laughed that hard since I was sixteen years old.

I eventually rented a truck, and then another one, just not that day.

Sometimes it's the stuff you don't think to worry about that bites you in the ass.

{ 9 }

A WAY OUT

A PROBLEM ARISES INVOLVING the phones and an unhappy customer. Geoff's sister, who now works with us at Legacy, blames the incident on me. She thinks I'm stupid, a dim bulb; I consider her a pathological liar. Sitting behind her desk, she points one finger at me and calls me a "fucking idiot," a description she uses every chance she gets. Incensed, I storm out of her office, retreating around the corner into the office that Geoff and I share. Upset that I've been blamed for something I haven't done, degraded by someone other than Geoff, I let out a primal scream and burst into tears. I have no idea how to contain my raging emotions. Geoff will take his sister's side, come down on me hard, and I can't cope with the injustice of it all. I grab the first thing I can get my hands on, the Rolodex on my desk, and throw it with all my might against the wall. I've had it with life, with Geoff's intrusive family, with him.

Then Geoff strolls into the office, just as casually as you please, a look of total relaxation on his face. He stands at my desk a moment or two, looking at me as if curious. The next thing I know, he grabs me by the face, as if it were a bowling ball, and slams it full force against the wall. I can hear the loud crack, the thud of meat meeting drywall. I stumble across the shattered Rolodex stand, the white cards strewn across the linoleum. Before I can recover my balance, Geoff picks me up by the scruff of my neck and throws me across the desk, sending the computer and file holders and phone crashing onto the floor. It sounds as if a dozen waiters have dropped their service trays simultaneously, so loud is the clatter. I lay there dazed, blinking. I don't think to cry, such is my shock. Then Geoff draws his leg back as far as it will swing and lands the toe of his shoe between my ribs. Before I can curl into a fetal position, he spits in my face. Once he's through, he turns on his heel and sashays out of the office. His sister never comes in.

When I finally get up, I grab a notebook and pen and lock myself in the bathroom. I sit on the edge of the toilet and cry and cry. I just can't take it anymore. We started the day excited and cheerful because we're all set to go on a much-needed vacation to Aruba, a pre-wedding getaway. We've been working so hard for so long that it's a big deal to be taking time off and going away. And here I am, once again, crying. I'm forever crying in this bathroom. I cry when Geoff calls me a worthless, stupid cunt. I cry when he picks me up, shoves me against a wall, and punches me in the face. His favorite trick is throwing me into the recycled-paper bin, like the piece of garbage we both believe I am. He never says, "I'm sorry," never acts as if he's done anything wrong. It's gotten so I believe that I somehow deserve the treatment. Each time, I get up, escape to the bathroom, wipe off the blood and tears, then go right back out there for more.

But today, instead, I write a letter to God. "I can't do this anymore. But I don't know what to do." I scribble these two sentences over and over again. Then I add, "This is my fault. I did something wrong in my life and this is the price I have to pay."

I really can't figure out what I've done to deserve heartache and abuse, but that doesn't seem to matter because I'm paying right through the nose. I reach for my nose, small as it is, feel around the edges, decide it isn't broken, then turn back to God.

As I write and cry some more, I hear a horn beeping. I say out loud, "I hope this is you, God, because I can't do this anymore."

When Geoff starts banging on the bathroom door, I tear the letter off the notepad, ball it up, and shove it into the trash can as far down as it will go.

That night, as we pack our bags for Aruba, he laughs and sings some made-up vacation song. "We're going on vacation, let's be happy!" Then he gives me a big bear hug. I just cry some more.

Learn to pray and rely on faith when you can't figure a way out yourself.

{ 10 }

THE TROUBLE
WITH DRIVERS

N OW HERE'S SOMETHING you may not realize: With trucks come drivers. With drivers come complications. Lots of complications. Unexpected, sometimes scary complications.

A drivers' association started up. Drivers would belong to the association—someone like me could register them—and the association would give them workers' comp as well as issue them a 1099, deeming them a true IC (independent contractor). The arrangement promised to save courier companies like mine a lot of paperwork, money, and time, so I'd been thrilled to discover it. One less pile of papers to go through each week with Mom, I concluded.

Sitting in my tiny office overlooking the graveyard, eating my bologna-and-cheese sandwich, I heard a knock at the door. Before I had a chance to answer, in came two huge, six-foot-five men. Next to me, they looked like twin Eiffel Towers in dark suits. One was from the FBI and the other was from the FBI Unit for the State Department for Workers' Compensation. The sight of them made my knees knock. I'd worried about bouncing checks and dog attacks, but I sensed these two could do a whole lot worse.

I ran my eyes over them to see if they were carrying firearms or handcuffs, just in case they felt inclined to use them. What I was in trouble for, I had no idea. An assortment of possibilities streamed through my head: Geoff had sicced them on me for his entertainment, I was about to be charged with tax evasion, a driver I'd somehow offended had filed a complaint. My head swirled.

After I invited them to sit down, they began questioning me about the company and my drivers. Apparently, the way I'd registered them wasn't legal. Of course, I didn't know that. I can laugh now, but if you could have seen me eating my bologna-and-cheese sandwich, scared to death, shaking and crying, you would have thought the world was coming to an end. Instead of pulling out a weapon or cuffing me, the two agents said, "It's not your fault, we understand."

"I only have a couple drivers. My payroll is $200 a week," I added, just in case they changed their minds.

I'd been excited by the prospect of not having to deal with workers' comp or issuing 1099s, handing that responsibility over to a drivers' association, but I realized that such conveniences involved far more hoops than a three-ring circus. If something looks too good to be true, it often is—another lesson I had to learn over and over again. I immediately canceled the association's services and went back to doing what I'd done before. At least the mistakes I was pretty sure I was making before hadn't brought the FBI down on my head.

Even without the government knocking at my door, managing drivers was an endless source of stress. Not just managing the reams of paperwork associated with them and paying them on time, but also getting them to do the job well. I've stressed over every single delivery my company has made, whether it was me making the delivery or a driver I'd hired. I wanted to take every job that was offered, and I wanted every single delivery to be perfect, without any issues, and I would bend over backward for every client. The stress of perfectionism got so bad that my mom went out and bought me a special stress relief lotion to put on my temples. "Honey," she said, "you worry way too much." But no amount of cream could relieve the angst created by hapless drivers.

I still remember the very first delivery that went all wrong, nearly driving me to an early grave. Paula, my mom's friend and our part-time employee, had arranged for me to recruit her husband as a driver. I was all about keeping things in the family, sharing an opportunity with insiders.

All was fine until the day Paula's husband couldn't find the delivery address to drop off a package. He'd had no issue finding the pickup spot, which was half the job, but the drop-off point, well, that eluded him. So what did he do when he couldn't find the building listed on the manifest? He chose not to sweat the small stuff, and instead went to lunch. What was an hour? he no doubt asked himself while ordering a sit-down meal.

The customer, used to important packages being delivered on time, kept calling the office to complain. "I was told the thing would be here by noon. Where the hell is it?" Each time he called, his aggravation grew to a whole new level. "You goddamn people are totally incompetent. I'm going to make sure you never darken my doorstep again." Being a people pleaser, I tried to appease him, but the only thing the man wanted, and rightly so, was his package.

We didn't have cell phones then, so I ran to the parking lot, jumped in my car, and drove around town trying to locate

Paula's missing husband so I could deliver the package myself, and maybe salvage a little goodwill into the bargain. Hours later, he came back to the office, package in hand, but by then I was out scouring the streets like a madwoman.

In the end, I had to let him go because I couldn't afford enough stress lotion to make that arrangement work.

But it wasn't just lackadaisical drivers; I had a long line of odd ducks who created headaches for me in an assortment of ways.

For about three years, I had a driver we called Dogman. Dogman lived in his van with two dogs. He was the best driver I'd ever had, because he was truly 24/7. I could call him at 2 a.m., and he'd roll out of his van ready to go, albeit with dog hair hanging off his beard and on his clothes. Katie, who eventually quit her managerial job and came back to work for me, would bring him coats and shirts so he wouldn't look like a bum while representing the company. He told her that he didn't like the shirts because they had stripes, or logos on the breast pocket, or buttons on the collar. Dogman, it seemed, was far too discerning.

One day, Dogman parked his delivery van in front of a very distinguished customer's house and left the engine idling for a good long time. Apparently, the sight of a weird man lurking in a parked van so scared the customer's wife that she phoned the cops. No sooner had he gotten out of his van, package in hand, than Dogman was confronted by two police officers in a cruiser, spread-eagled across the hood, and frisked for hidden weapons. All the time, his dogs threw themselves against the passenger window, barking maniacally. Dogman quit after that, figuring we'd all be better off.

Then there was Mark. When making a delivery for one of my biggest customers, he decided to relieve himself on their front lawn. The customer's mother, roughly ninety years old, who happened to be looking out the window, complained that she'd seen his penis. Try taking that call.

Mary, the chain-smoker, was the next in a long lineup of problem drivers. When she turned in paperwork, we had to leave it in the other room because you could smell the smoke off her manifests. One time we sent her to pick up a white rabbit for a delivery—it was going to be used for a TV commercial—and we were sure the thing would turn yellow or die from smoke inhalation.

I also had a driver, Carl, who, at forty years old, would go home every day and have lunch with his mother. The woman would call me whenever he was a minute late coming home, just to make sure he hadn't been hit by a car.

Steve literally had a memory-loss problem. If he forgot to take his memory pill, which happened quite a lot, he would forget what he was doing, which is bad if you're supposed to be delivering packages in a timely manner.

And then of course there was Charlie. In his mid-sixties, Charlie wore cut-off short shorts with a white tank top. His balls would hang out of his shorts, which made everyone in the office cringe.

These were the people who represented me. In this business, that's pretty much what you get. Despite the growing pains associated with building a trucking fleet and managing drivers, I was beginning to realize I had the capacity to spin straw into gold. I was dedicated and gave a personal touch that others didn't. It wouldn't be long before I gave my competition a real run for their money.

Growing your company brings more opportunities and bigger complications. Expect change and embrace that the more you take on, more is expected.

———————————

{ 11 }

PING-PONG
IN ARUBA

WE GET UP and catch our flight to Aruba as though nothing has happened, but something has shifted for me. I've reached a breaking point after the fight at Legacy. The vacation, unsurprisingly, only brings more grief. After settling into our hotel room, we meet up with Geoff's best friend, Kevin, a vulgar, fat forty-something who makes Geoff seem kind and generous by comparison. Wendy, Kevin's wife, is also along for the ride. Frail and thin, she flinches every time Kevin calls her by her proper name. Like me, she's used to being called "cunt." The couple's four children are grown. Empty nesters, Wendy and Kevin have nothing better to do than hang around with us.

The men decide that we should take a tour of the island. We hop in the rental car, the men in the front seat, the women in the back, and head down the main road. Passing by sandy white beaches, palm trees, and magnificent estates, Kevin is inspired to speak. "We're going to buy a place here," he crows.

I happen to know that they're broke, that they can't afford this trip let alone a multi-million-dollar mansion, but I know enough to keep my mouth shut.

Wendy says, "Oh, yeesh, Kevin, I don't think we can afford it."

Kevin flips around, his rage barely contained, and tells her to shut the fuck up. He calls her a stupid cunt. "You're such an idiot. Don't you dare say another word on this fucking tour."

I think, *Thank God I don't get treated that way. She's so much worse off than me.*

Later that afternoon, after Kevin and Wendy have gone off on their own, Geoff demands that I play Ping-Pong with a random couple we've just met in the lobby. He's been flirting with every pretty girl we've come across, so I'm sure that the minute I leave him alone he'll get one of their phone numbers and arrange for a hookup. I say to him, not wanting to turn my back on him for that long, "I don't really want to play."

"Cunt, what's wrong with you?" he says, right in front of the couple. "You're a bitch, and if I say you're going to play Ping-Pong, you're going to play fucking Ping-Pong."

The poor girl is mortified. She looks at her partner, begs him with her eyes to get her out of here.

We end up playing together because Geoff won't let up until we do. I feel so bad, so ashamed, because I know she's horrified by the interaction. I can see my situation clearly through her eyes.

After, I sit in an empty bar with my head on the long, cool surface, sobbing. *There's no way out of this. There's no way out.* I cry because I don't know how I'll ever get out of this relationship. I'm so obsessed with Geoff, despite his abuse. I'm no longer in love with him, but I don't have any options. I am living completely through him. And now, heading into a marriage with him, I'm setting myself up for more of the same.

*You can often see more clearly
through the eyes of a stranger.*

_____

{ 12 }

HIJACKERS

E WERE GROWING so fast we couldn't hire enough help to keep up with the workflow. This would have been a great problem to be confronting unless, like me, you couldn't afford more staff, and the staff you did have were burning out fast.

I suddenly found myself with a shortage of drivers. I couldn't keep them long enough because, what with the booming economy of the late nineties, all the other courier companies were scooping them up to meet their own needs. We competed by offering big signing bonuses, so drivers bounced around from one company to the other, leaving us all perpetually in the lurch. Sign up for a month with one company, get their bonus, and then jump to another—that was how the game was played. Companies overpaid not just drivers but all their employees. A potential candidate could walk into almost any place, quote their asking price, and be paid it, if not more. Kids were exiting college and writing their own meal tickets.

I hired Gary as a driver in this highly competitive atmosphere. When he didn't immediately jump ship to take advantage of other signing bonuses, I brought him into the office, thinking him honorable and loyal. In no time, I made him my first full-time dispatcher, even though he had no experience. Mom and I taught him everything the job entailed: recruiting drivers, assigning them jobs, doing the associated paperwork, and so on.

Gary worked from 7 a.m. until 3:30 p.m. Monday through Friday, opening the office each morning, and keeping the place running for at least an hour before everyone else showed up to do their jobs. For the first time in three years, I enjoyed the luxury of putting my mascara on at home in the bathroom mirror, as opposed to swiping it on in a dark car in the wee hours of the morning at some stoplight. It was such a relief to sleep in, to sip my tea and read the paper while the sun rose, before charging ahead with my day, all cylinders firing. Thank God for Gary; I'd hit the jackpot when I'd hired him.

As time went on, however, Gary began to come in late. First, it was fifteen minutes, no big deal, and then thirty, then fifty. I would never have known about his increasing tardiness had my customers not called me to complain about having to ring multiple times just to place their deliveries. Odd. Why wasn't Gary showing up at the office when he said he was? I spoke to him about the matter a couple of times, reminded him how important it was that he get in on time to answer the phones. He seemed contrite, swore he'd never be late again, and I completely forgot about the issue, never thinking that's how these things start.

Then one day Gary was late again. After receiving yet another customer complaint, I called to tell him how unhappy I was. I hated to press the issue, but with customers griping, I had no choice. Threaten my business, and I will take a stand. This time, instead of being remorseful, Gary yelled back at me, told me he quit, and then slammed down the phone. I stood in my front hallway with the receiver in one hand, my car keys in the other, unsure as to what had just happened. Had I been too harsh, too demanding? I prided myself on being good to my people, but maybe I'd let my annoyance get the better of me. I could have kicked myself. I had my own apartment, which I shared with another girl; a new office that didn't overlook a graveyard; and a modicum of time to breathe, pursue a social life, and date a little, but now I felt as if I was right back to square one, minus a noisy washing machine thrumming in the background. I'd have to go back to being on the desk by 7 a.m., which wouldn't be so bad if I didn't work until 7 p.m., and if I weren't on call 24/7. I'd even been on the cusp of joining a gym, spending some time on my physical well-being instead of running myself straight into the ground, but now that wasn't going to happen. I refused to be the fool with a beeper on her gym pants, running on the treadmill or participating in a class, constantly having to bail to address yet another emergency. A couple of weeks of that, and I'd be the most despised person in step aerobics, forced to slink out the door with my beeping tail between my legs.

I was sitting in dispatch early one morning when a customer dialed me up. Apparently, he'd received a price sheet from another courier company that looked an awful lot like mine, which he found curious. I asked him to fax it over, so I could give it a look. I watched the first page come over the fax, and sure enough, it *was* my price sheet, only with "Xpressman" whited out of the header. There was Gary's name typed over it. I felt a cold, hard knot of rage form in my belly. I'd taught Gary the ropes, moved him rapidly up the ladder, entrusted him with a lot of responsibility, and here he was, stealing my work product. My customer then proceeded to fax me over my entire set of sales literature, items I'd spent the last few years polishing, all with Gary's name on them. The bastard had stolen my customer list, my brochures, and my price sheets. He'd copied everything while he'd been alone in the office; done a mass mailing as well, probably on my dime. He'd up and quit like that not because I'd overstepped my boundaries, but because he'd pirated enough of my business to launch his own. The old Michelle would have curled up in a corner and wailed; the new Michelle wanted blood.

I hired a lawyer. It didn't take long, however, to realize that there was nothing to be done because I hadn't had Gary sign a non-compete agreement. In an employee-favoring market, employers didn't bother with such details because they were grateful for the opportunity to hire someone. Or so I'd thought. I vowed I would never make that rookie mistake again, dismissing basic requirements out of desperation, latching on to someone just because he seemed to have chosen me over the rest of his suitors.

I was sure I'd lose my business to Gary. One by one, my customers would abandon my sinking ship. If Gary had the capacity to shank me in the back, court my customers with my pricing and materials, who knew how far he would go to ruin me? He'd no doubt seen a naive young woman ripe for the pillaging, a sweetie pie who had no business operating in a cutthroat industry. I could picture him snickering about my high heels, short skirts, and girlish voice over a few beers with the boys. They'd all laugh about how easy it was for the wolf to take down the deer. Gone were the days when kindhearted people would cut me some slack because I didn't know what I was doing; now I had to watch myself lest others use my weaknesses against me.

I tried to hold steady, to tell myself that this was just another bump in the road. After all, Xpressman offered a great service to customers. Good service begets loyalty; I'd always banked on that. Those who decided to go elsewhere, namely with Gary, weren't worth keeping anyway. I figured karma would do its thing: Gary would end up trusting someone else only to get the rug pulled out from underneath him. My job was to work even harder and keep my eye on the ball, to learn from my mistakes. Which didn't stop me from making even more.

Sometimes it's harder to trust ourselves than it is to trust others.

———————

{ 13 }

SMALL FAVORS

AFTER WE RETURNED from Aruba, I got into a car accident. We had just got this beautiful, brand-new Mercedes. A woman stopped short, causing me to run straight into her. I was terrified to tell Geoff, but I needed to rent a replacement car.

"You don't deserve that car," he says, when he learns what happened. "You're not worthy of that car." The accident wasn't my fault, but you can't tell him that.

That night, after screaming at me about the car, Geoff doesn't come home. Upset, I drive around looking for him at his favorite haunts. Five or six hours pass, and I don't know where to head, I just know I'll be damned if I'm going to arrive home before him. I can't go to my parents, not after what I've put them through, what I've forced them to accept. I can't keep hurting them that way. I don't have any friends to go to at this point. I've ignored even my best friends, Shea and Juls, for so long in favor of focusing on Geoff that I can't turn to them. I've neglected them because I'm afraid to leave his side for fear of him cheating on me. Finally, at around three o'clock in the morning, I go home, defeated. I doze off on the floor, hoping to hear his key in the lock, his footstep on the carpet.

At eight o'clock the next morning, Geoff strolls through the door as if nothing is amiss. He looks freshly showered. "Where were you?" I wail. "Why didn't you come home?" I know that he wasn't hanging out with the guys, which is the excuse he gives me, and I say as much.

Then he says, after admitting he had some fun with a girl in her dorm room, "It's over. You need to move out."

I shake my head in disbelief. It's been exactly three days since we got back from Aruba, three weeks since we moved in together, three years since we started Legacy Signs together, six years of dating, and *bam*, Geoff is breaking up with me. Despite the on-again, off-again pattern we established, I can't believe he wants out.

Jealousy drains out of me like water through a sieve. This time, it isn't just Geoff I stand to lose, but the roof over my head, a vehicle I adore, my job, my entire social circle. "Where am I going to go? I don't know where I'm going to live, I don't have a job, where am I going to work?"

He says, "I'll pay you a weekly salary until you find work. After all, you did help me start Legacy."

I feel a surge of hope. He won't know how to handle it all without me. I run the whole back office; I'm his right-hand person. He'll need to hire somebody or face disaster. He'll come running back to me, just wait.

He takes a shower while I weep outside the door. Then he picks up some stuff from his dresser—a fresh shirt, a change of underwear, jeans—and leaves.

I remain wrapped in a blanket on the floor in my pajamas. I rip up all our pictures, the pieces of which are scattered around me.

Geoff calls my sister Gina and says, "You better come get her. She's a complete wreck."

When Gina comes inside, she finds me on the living room floor, dazed. I keep going back and forth between asking her why he's breaking up with me and crying. "I need to talk to him."

Gina calls Shea, my mother, and my auntie, saying, "She's really a mess. She's in trouble. We need to get her."

Once the women gather, they throw my clothes in trash bags, toss them in the car, and come back for me. "Michelle, you gotta move, you gotta get up," one of them says. When I can't, one of them grabs me under my armpits, another grabs my legs, and they carry me out that door, still wrapped in a blanket, and toss me in the back of the car.

They drive me to Gina and Shea's apartment. They plop me down on that couch and I lay there, sobbing.

For days, I don't eat or drink, I just cry.

Sometimes the thing you fear most is the best thing that can happen to you.

{ 14 }

EXTORTIONISTS

I WAS DOING SOME deliveries for a company when I ran across Crystal working the front desk. She was an older lady, probably in her late fifties, whom I'd known from my days at Legacy. We'd been friendly back then, so I was always happy to connect with her on the phone from time to time when arranging deliveries for her employer. We'd exchange a bit of gossip or an encouraging word before hanging up and getting on with our day.

One day Crystal called me at the office, told me she'd lost her job, and asked me if I was recruiting. I didn't have any positions open at that moment and told her as much. A month or so later she checked back with me, saying she was out of money and desperate for a job. Remembering how hard it had been for me after Geoff had kicked me to the curb, I decided to create a job for her. I figured I could always use some help answering phones, taking in orders, things like that, so I hired her, no questions asked.

Of course, Crystal was thrilled. She settled in at our front desk and carried on as if she'd always been part of the gang.

A month or so after Crystal's arrival, Katie noticed cash missing from her drawer, which had never happened before. We often did COD in which drivers brought back cash to the office. It was kept in the top drawer of Katie's desk in our reception area, where Crystal sat, until the next trip to the bank. It was a small amount that had disappeared, something like $20, but Katie was pretty sure it was supposed to be there. The two of us scratched our heads as we tried to figure out where it had gone or who might have taken it. Had Mom needed it for petty cash? No, she said. Could the guy who came in to scan documents for us at night be the culprit? Maybe. The drawer was never locked, because we had no reason to lock it. We treated the incident like a mystery, no big deal, and quickly forgot it.

The following week, we discovered another $50 missing from the drawer after a cash delivery. The week after that, $40 vanished. Three times in a row meant this was no oversight or coincidence. Someone was palming money, which left me feeling completely violated. Who would take anything from me? Why? I'd help anyone in need; all he or she had to do was ask. Thanks to Geoff, I knew precisely what it felt like to beg for money, so I'd made it clear that folks could come to me if they needed a temporary loan or some extra help to see them through a pinch. Hurt and disgusted, I decided it was time to take matters into my own hands. Over the weekend, I installed a video camera. The lens pointed directly at the front desk.

On Monday morning, I planted $30 in the cash drawer. Sure enough, by Friday evening it was gone. I took the tape home and slipped it into the VCR on Saturday morning. I had to fast-forward through three days of tape before discovering my thief.

I picked up the phone and dialed Katie to tell her that the mystery had been solved. I'd caught Crystal red-handed. There she was, sneaking into Katie's top desk drawer, grabbing the money, covering it up in her hand, and sliding it into her purse, which she'd positioned below. A little while later, she got up and went back to Katie's desk, again with purse in hand. This time she emptied the lower drawer of its pencils and pens. I have to admit, that last act of kleptomania made me laugh—a temporary relief from my disappointment and disgust.

"I can't believe it," Katie said. "I knew it! I knew something wasn't right with Crystal."

On Monday, I asked Katie to come into my office for some moral support. Helping people has always made me feel good. I hate seeing others unhappy or upset. Worse, confrontation makes me want to head for the hills or, at the very least, hide under my desk. Unfortunately, there was no way around what I had to do.

When I called Crystal into my office, I asked her outright if she'd been stealing from the front desk.

She said no.

I then offered her another chance to tell me the truth. Half of me was horrified to be having the conversation; the other was curious how she would handle the situation in light of the proof I held.

"I would never steal from you," she said, without skipping a beat. "You gave me a job. I've known you for so long. I'm not a thief—I would never do something like that."

I studied her impassive face, amazed at her ability to lie through her teeth. I was dealing with someone with a completely different makeup. Me? I'd be on my knees groveling for mercy, if I could ever spit in the face of such generosity to begin with. I'd help everyone if I could—financially, emotionally, physically. If I had to run around with ten screaming kids all day long so some mother could enjoy a day off, I would. If I had to give out $20 and keep only $2 for myself, I would. Gladly. It's my nature. I am my mother's daughter. But I'd had just about enough of contractors—contractors I'd only ever been kind to—ripping me off with impunity. I could tolerate idiosyncrasies—dog hair all over a driver's clothes or living with mommy at the age of forty—or a lack of polish, or mishaps now and again, but not this kind of treachery.

"Stop lying. You're just embarrassing yourself. I have the tape right here that proves you're the thief." I pointed to the tape I'd set at the edge of my desk. The very sight of it would have scared me straight, had me blurting out a confession. But not Crystal.

She denied it.

"I'd be more than happy to play the tape for you if you'd like." I picked the tape up and headed to the far corner, where I kept the VCR for training purposes. I flicked the TV on, muted the volume. I looked at her, wondering how far she would make me go.

Again, Crystal denied her guilt.

Just as I was about to slide the tape into the VCR, Crystal cracked.

"I'm so sorry," she said, covering her face with both hands, letting out a low, thin howl. Her tearful display somehow felt contrived. I thought I knew her, but just how little I did scared the tar out of me. I suddenly felt cold, as if every window had been left open to the elements during the night. I couldn't run my company on my own, or grow it with the help of loyal relatives alone, but how could I trust others, or my instincts, after this? How could I have been so wrong?

I told Crystal she was fired. She offered no reason, no excuse for her behavior. I walked her straight to the front door, opened it for her, and watched until she pulled her car out of the parking lot. I couldn't care less what she'd left on her desk; it was probably stuff she had stolen from me anyhow. I remembered the box of belongings I had carted out of Legacy that last day: a pair of shoes, my new Rolodex, an old family photo. I felt equally angry and defeated.

Shortly after I canned Crystal, I received a notice from the unemployment office. Crystal had applied to receive benefits after losing her job. Incredulous, I arranged a conference call with unemployment and then sent them the tape to demonstrate why I'd been forced to let her go, why I shouldn't have to pay her benefits. Extortion! Normally, I would never want to strip someone of her ability to earn a living, but this was too much, even for a people pleaser like me. Crystal's claim was denied, and I never heard from her again.

Help others, but don't
expect payment in kind; just
do it if it feels right.

{ 15 }

ADDICTION THERAPY

I MISS GEOFF. I have no idea what I'm going to do with my life. I'm twenty-three years old, I haven't gone to college, and I'm unemployed.

But it isn't the grief over losing Geoff that causes me to cry; I'm mourning the loss of myself. I've become so dependent on another person that I have no sense of my identity. Without Geoff, I'm nothing. He told me that a million times, and I believe it.

Yet I've got an inkling, deep down, that my prayers have been answered, that I've found a way out. God found my note buried in that garbage pail. I've been given a second chance, though I haven't a clue what I'll do with it.

It doesn't take long for my parents to recognize that I need to talk to someone. I go from 105 pounds to ninety-five in no time flat, again. I refuse to consume anything but tea. All of this, by the way, isn't anything new. Whenever Geoff breaks up with me, which he does every six months, I refuse to eat.

My uncle, a probation officer, knows of a therapist, a drug addiction specialist. My parents can think of no other option and say, "That will do."

A week later, I find myself sitting in a chair across from Susan the therapist.

It takes me two sessions before I can finally speak. My first words are, "I just want to call him. Can I please call him?"

She says, "You can do anything you want to do, but let me just ask you, why do you want to call him?"

"Because if I call him, I'll be okay."

"Well, when was the last time you talked to him?"

It's been a whole week at this point.

She says, "Okay, you've gone one week without calling him. I know you feel terrible right now, but how will you feel when you do call him?"

"I'm gonna feel great when I call him." This I say through snot and tears, barely able to take a breath. "It would make me happy just to hear his voice."

"Well, how long would that make you happy for?"

"I don't know, maybe forty-five minutes."

"Okay. After you talked to him, then felt happy for forty-five minutes, what would happen after that?"

"I'd start to get sad again. The feelings of loneliness would come back and make me feel empty again." I sigh, hearing what I'm saying.

"Well, you've gone a full week without talking to him. Now you want to talk to him, and if you do, then you're going to have to go back through all this pain you've just gone through for the whole week. Do you really want to go back through that pain again?"

I say, "No, I don't."

"Then let's take this one hour at a time. Let's get through the hour without calling him, and after you get through that hour, let's work on the next one."

And so I do. I take it hour by hour, bargaining with myself, *If I can just make it through this hour and not call him, I'll be okay.* And then the next hour comes and I want to call him, and I tell myself, *No, I just got through the last hour. I've got to get through one more.*

I know that I have to break free of Geoff. I know he's bad for me, like heroin. I know I'm powerless, that I can't resist his draw. My therapist gave me a tool called the Power and Control Wheel, put out by the National Center on Domestic and Sexual Violence. She presented it to me when I told her that Geoff wasn't abusive toward me in the beginning, only in the later years when he hit me. There it all was in the form of a pie chart, everything I'd lived through, so clearly laid out in black and white. Emotional abuse. Physical abuse. Economic abuse. Isolation from friends and family. And on and on. Even though I understand this on an intellectual level, I still want him. I can't help myself.

One day after therapy, as I head home to my sister's apartment, I suddenly find myself going in the opposite direction. Before I know it, I'm in the parking lot of St. Joseph's church. I go in and sit in a pew. *Please, God, make it better. Please make me happy. I love him. I want him. I need him. Please, please make me happy.* Obviously, I think "happy" means being with Geoff. I think things will be better if we're back together. Even so, I beg God to make it better.

**Remember that the path forward
is one step after another.**

{ 16 }

A WOLF IN SHEEP'S CLOTHING

I WAS AT MY desk going through e-mails when I tripped over a message from someone named Bob Nichols. The name didn't ring a bell. I clicked to open and read the single, strange line: "You're hot." After years of insults—*you're ugly, you're too skinny, you look disgusting*—the fact that anybody found me sexy lit me up.

I smoothed my hair and fiddled with the top button of my blouse, barely aware I was doing so. All I needed was one of my staff to pass my office and catch me all starry-eyed. It would be just my luck if Tom, my new dispatcher, chose this very moment to poke his head in to say hello and see how things were going. His office was in the front of the building; mine was in the back, next to the bathrooms, which meant not only did I see Tom every time he had to use the john, but I also spent the day listening to people peeing. Tom had a bad habit of taking the seat across from me, making himself comfortable in my office, and chit-chatting, which was nearly as off-putting as the unavoidable bathroom noises emanating through the dividing wall. It's not that I didn't like my people; I just didn't have time for small talk. I glanced out my office door. No one was there. I looked at the computer screen again, at the name of my secret admirer. Still no clue. I'd been dating a fellow I did deliveries for, a man I had an awful crush on, but there was no way he would have sent me this note under an assumed name. He didn't operate that way, play games. Over our first lunch he'd told me he was dating someone—nothing serious, just dating—and I'd admired his honesty. A refreshing change from Geoff. I was actually allowing myself to contemplate marrying this guy. And yet this note captured my attention, my imagination. *Someone thinks I'm hot, but who?*

An hour or so later, another e-mail: "I think ur sexy." I noted the lack of capitalization, the sudden use of the abbreviation. *Okay, who is this? Is this someone I know playing a joke on me?* This time I found myself getting nervous, if not a little creeped out. I looked out the window to see if anybody was standing out there with a camera to capture my reaction. Nothing. I typed back: "Who is this?" I stared at the screen as I waited for the response. The phone rang once, then again, and suddenly I was so busy with the workday I forgot about the odd messages.

A couple of days later, I was sifting through some regular staff correspondence. Katie had pricing questions, Charlie wanted to give me an update on drivers, Tom let me know that he might have to leave early since his wife had to work late and he'd need to be home to cover their three kids. Nothing unusual. Then, *bam*, up sprang another e-mail from Bob Nichols. This time the note was devoid of all charm: "i want to rip ur clothes off and have sex with u on your desk."

I blinked, sure I had somehow misinterpreted the note, what with the abbreviations. I pushed myself away from my desk, the very desk someone imagined the two of us on, and winced when I realized I hadn't been mistaken. I didn't know how I should feel—afraid, angry, or a combination of both emotions. I'd been dealing with aggressive men for a lot of years, there was no escaping it in a male-dominated industry, so I knew the best way to respond was with a show of force; otherwise, I'd be eaten alive.

"I'm not sure who this is, but knock it off." I would have to mind my step when I headed to the parking lot that evening in case someone was waiting for me in the shadows.

A couple of weeks passed without incident. Almost as soon as I began to feel that Bob Nichols was no longer an issue, my computer blinked with not one but four e-mails in a row. *Bing, bing, bing, bing.*

"ur fucking hot."

"i want to rip ur clothes off."

"i can't stop thinking about u."

The fourth one took on an ominous tone. It began with threats, a description of what he would do to me if he got the chance. Then he called me a "stuck-up bitch." Who the fuck did I think I was, he demanded to know.

My hands shook as I deleted the e-mails. It didn't occur to me to call the cops. What were they supposed to do? Station an officer by my door, interrogate my friends and neighbors, set up a trap on the Internet? I kept the e-mails to myself, not wanting to share them with my mother, my auntie, or the guy I was dating. I was now the strong one, the one people depended on; I didn't want to worry them or make them think I couldn't handle myself.

Again, I got busy handling the day-to-day running of a growing business. There was always a stack of tasks that needed attending to. Case in point: Tom the dispatcher had given me his two weeks' notice. His wife had received a big promotion and they'd decided he was going to leave the workforce and be a stay-at-home dad. We were all sad to see him go. He was a hard worker, funny, and got the job done. Sure, he could be a pain, what with his sticking his head into my office any ol' time he wanted. And there was that time he'd overstepped, asked me if I had any cute girlfriends. The question had taken me aback. I'd hesitated before speaking, and then said, "First of all, you're married. And second, I'm your boss. I'd appreciate if you'd refrain from asking me such things." Putting his hands up over his head as if to surrender, he'd said, "I'm sorry. I won't let it happen again." And I'd let bygones be bygones. Water under the bridge.

I now had to go out and find his replacement, which meant placing an ad in the paper. Dispatcher was one of the hardest jobs to fill. Katie, Mom, or I would have to work from 7 a.m. until 7 p.m. to train someone for two or three months straight. Don't get me wrong, we were used to working those hours, but by this point we'd all paid our dues. And I now had a man waiting for me at home.

I was typing away on a job quote when I got another Bob Nichols e-mail: "hey who do u think u r?" Instead of typing back, I stopped dead in my tracks and looked closely at the e-mails. This time, something niggled at me.

Oda Mae. Oda Mae Brown is what my friends used to call me, after Whoopi Goldberg's character in the movie *Ghost*. Oda Mae could predict things and pick up on things other characters couldn't. Like Oda Mae, I had a sharp sixth sense. I could read the wind, pick up on other people's energy, and smell trouble before it reared its ugly head. I often knew what was about to happen when everyone else was clueless. Once, shortly after she'd arrived home from shopping, my best friend Shea's boyfriend Gary had stopped by to break up with her. She called me, bawling her eyes out. I had a gut feeling that I couldn't explain. I said, "I think Gary is dating someone and I think it's someone we know." Shocked and angry—because she knew I was probably right; after all, I am Oda Mae Brown—she called Gary, only to discover that I'd been right. Intuition was a parlor trick I tended to ignore because I wanted to believe what people told me, even if it meant ignoring my gut.

I looked at the message again. My nose twitched. "i want to rip ur clothes off... what do u think about that? i find u sexy and u know who this is! it is right underneath ur nose."

Then it came to me. I minimized this latest e-mail and pulled up one from my dispatcher Tom, who had just quit.

"hi michelle, just checking in to see how ur doing?"

Sure enough, he had used the same style of writing: everything in lowercase, those same abbreviations. As I went back and forth between Bob Nichols's e-mails and Tom the dispatcher's, I knew my gut feeling was right. He *was* right beneath my nose, someone I knew and trusted. Bob Nichols and Tom the dispatcher were one and the same.

A wave of nausea rose in my throat. The hairs on my forearms stood on end. The guy had worked for me; I'd seen him every day, interacted with him every day. He'd sent me dirty e-mails then walked down the hall to say hi and see if there was anything I wanted for lunch, as if butter wouldn't melt. He'd been studying me, watching me, gauging me, and I hadn't even noticed. I felt violated, as if he'd walked into my bedroom while I was asleep, pulled back my covers, and ran his hands over my naked body without causing me to stir. What else was I missing? Who else was waiting to pounce on me?

Then I got mad. How dare he kick my knees out from beneath me? How dare he betray my trust? How dare he make me doubt myself, and everyone I knew?

"Tom, I know this is you," I typed as fast as my fingers would go. "You better knock it off or I'm going to go to the police, and call your wife." I envisioned calling his wife for a second, telling her that her husband wasn't the man she thought he was, that he was playing her for a fool. I'd be doing her a huge favor, even though I knew it wouldn't feel that way to her in the moment.

None of us wants to believe we can be replaced that easily by another woman. The thought of her pain extinguished my burning impulse for revenge.

"i am sorry, michelle, i just think u are beautiful and i am having a tough time in my marriage. i promise i won't do it again..."

I stared at Tom's response. I wanted people to find me beautiful, I really did. What I didn't want was harassment from a man I'd sunk time into and trusted as one of my own. What I didn't want was to feel preyed upon, threatened, disrespected, and tricked. I had a hard-enough time trusting others as it was. A wolf in sheep's clothing could set me back years.

On a sunny spring afternoon a few years later, an e-mail chimed on my cell phone. I pulled out my BlackBerry and found a message from someone named David Smith. The name didn't ring a bell. "Hey you, I saw you on Willowbrook the other day. You're looking hot."

Again, excited to think that someone out there thought I was hot—particularly since I'd married the man I'd been dating the last time I'd received such an e-mail, whom I was now in the midst of divorcing—I perked right up. *Wow, someone thinks I look hot.* So hungry was I for approval, I practically spun on my axis right there in my front yard. There was nothing like failure to make me feel unworthy and unattractive, especially as I was now the mother of two small children, which meant I slept about two hours a day. A boost like that would make me strut my stuff for at least thirty minutes. Then it occurred to me—I hadn't been on Willowbrook the other day. I hadn't lived on that street for two whole years, not since I'd sold my starter house and moved to my swanky new neighborhood, the very same neighborhood I'd dreamed of when I was dating Geoff. Had I visited one of my old neighbors recently? I had to stop and think.

Curiosity getting the better of me, I e-mailed back. "Who's this?" Maybe it was the guy I'd met at the last industry get-together, the suit and tie I'd slipped my card, or the fellow Shea had wanted me to meet. She was always trying to fix me up. A stream of pleasant possibilities flooded my mind.

"I am not telling," was the response I got, which sounded an immediate alarm. It couldn't be Tom the dispatcher. He'd been out of the picture for way too long. I'd nipped that issue. When no other e-mail followed, I slipped my cell phone back in my pocket and headed to the office. I had a number of new trucks that needed inspecting, a management meeting to preside over, a slew of customer calls I had to return. I didn't have time to play guessing games. This wasn't someone I wanted to meet anyway; my every instinct told me so.

A couple of days passed and I got another e-mail from David. "You are looking so good, what have you been up to? Why don't you meet me so you can see who this is?"

At this point, my need for safety far exceeded my desire for admiration. Besides, the message didn't sound flirtatious; it sounded vaguely creepy. Oda Mae kicked in. I studied each word on my cell phone screen, the writing style of this David. It was completely different from the one Bob had used before. Couldn't be him, despite the familiar feelings the message elicited. I responded, "No thanks and stop e-mailing me."

"who do you think you are, the queen of fucking england?"

I didn't notice the sudden lack of capitals in his sentence, so busy was I typing my reply. "Please don't e-mail me again."

"i want to have sex with you . . ." and on and on the immediate response went.

I knew right then it was Tom, because the final piece had clicked into place. No capitals. I shook my head in disbelief. The man wasn't a bumbling fool with a schoolboy's crush; he was dangerous, pathological. Before fear set in, I shot off a response. "Tom, I know this is you. You better knock it off." Calling him out on the tarmac had worked before; I hoped it would work again.

"who is this Tom dude? you think ur so great, so beautiful. ur a bitch, so full of yourself. u need to be put in your place."

With my sister along for moral support, I went to the police station in Braintree that evening. They took my story. The detective asked me to print out all the e-mails and bring them back the following day. I was nervous to go home. I assumed Tom knew where I lived. My dad had to come over and check out my house before I would go in.

Despite informing Tom that the police were now involved, the e-mails kept coming. He loved me, he wanted to make love to me, I was a bitch, he would show me who was boss. Geoff had beaten me with his fist, proven himself totally unpredictable, yet Tom with his incessant e-mails and schizophrenic messaging scared me even more.

The police department wanted to build a case. They needed time to subpoena all the e-mail accounts. I was afraid to show up at home, afraid I was being watched. Every horror movie I'd seen as a kid came back to haunt me. Hockey masks, chainsaws, blood, and gore.

One night, I got a particularly frightening e-mail. Tom talked about throwing me down on the desk, ripping my clothes off. His rage and aggression were palpable. From what he said, if he got a hold of me, he would make my experiences with Geoff seem like a playdate in comparison. I called the detective. He said he could call Tom or go down and confront him face to face. The detective then called Tom, told him he could either come to his house and confront him in front of his wife, or they could meet at the market down the street from where he lived. Tom chose the latter.

There, the detective explained to Tom that there were anti-stalking laws and that his e-mails could be traced. Tom admitted he'd been sending the e-mails and that he couldn't stop. He said he was in love with me and that he thought I liked the messages, a detail that, when recounted, freaked me out.

Shortly after the police confrontation, the phone rang. My sister answered. The man identified himself as the detective, explained he was calling to confirm my address. My sister gave it to him. When my sister told me about the call, I knew it had been Tom on the other end of the line. When I called the police station, they confirmed that they'd not placed the call.

There are still days when I think this is probably not really over.

Our insecurities create blind spots; our strengths allow us to see through them.

{ 17 }

REMEMBER THIS

AFTER SEVERAL WEEKS of living on my sister's couch, I decide to pick myself up and drag myself into the shower. It's been ages since I've changed my underwear, let alone bathed. Feeling pretty gross inside and out, I get it in my head, for no reason I can think of, that today will be the day I get my act together, make some decisions.

As if by divine mandate, I get dressed, jump in my car, and head to Legacy. Something inside me knows I'm tempting fate, but I have to see for myself if I can resist him. There's a chance Geoff will take me back when he sees me and how fragile I've become from grief; I'm not sure if I can turn him down. Like someone who's just owned up to their alcoholism, it's time for me to show up at the bar and see what will happen when I'm faced with temptation.

I have no idea what has possessed me, or what I'm going to say to Geoff. All I can do is cry. As I approach the warehouse, I tell myself, *Just go in, grab your stuff, and leave. Take a deep breath. You can do this.* I know I'm addicted to the relationship thanks to my work with Susan the therapist, but something inside me actually believes I can resist him.

I pull into the parking lot and immediately spot Geoff's car, a bright-red Mercedes that turns heads. With a deep breath, I get out of my vehicle, open the warehouse door, and go into the office we once shared. No one is there. I throw my belongings into a box. After working there for three years, ninety hours a week, everything I own fits neatly into one box. Everything else is his.

When I'm just about finished, Geoff walks in, all smiles. He doesn't appear the least bit surprised to find me here. He looks me up and down, all ninety pounds, complete with puffy, red eyes. The first thing he says is, "Where'd you get *that* outfit?" as if to cut me right down to size. There isn't a hint of sympathy or regret in his voice.

I just look at him, force a smile, and say, "I'm well, and you?"

"Really?" He raises an amused eyebrow.

"Really."

"So, what are you going to do now?" he asks. He finds this question amusing as well.

What am I going to do? I know I'll have nothing when I walk out the door, now that this last chance to get back together seems to have fizzled. I have no self-esteem, no home to call my own, no education. I barely have the confidence to take a pee by myself. Then I say, "I don't know. I don't know what I'm going to do."

He looks at me dead-on, with a smirk on his face, pointing at me between the eyes. He says, "Remember this: you'll never amount to anything without me."

I stand before him, feeling the full weight of his words. He doesn't want me back; I can see that. I get it—really get it. Part of me feels relieved, as though I've just dodged a bullet; the other part absorbs the information like a punch to the gut. I believe him, that I won't amount to anything, and yet I don't. I stand in front of him, with tears streaming down my face, and eventually I say, "Okay."

I take my stuff and walk out the door, knowing that I will never, ever go back.

I believe that somebody watches over us. I asked God for help, and this is the form it has taken. I can tell you right now that I don't like it. Instead of Geoff, what I've been given is the strength to walk away.

I jump in my car and tear out of the parking lot. I so badly want to drive off the road. I want to get in a car accident, so I won't have to live in my skin anymore. What *am* I going to do? What *am* I going to do with my life? I'm a nobody. I have nothing. I might as well crawl under a rock, because this is my rock bottom.

Driving down Canal Street, I chant to myself, *"You will never amount to anything without me. You will never amount to anything without me."* What am I, or can I be, without Geoff? He made me believe he did it all, that I've simply been along for the joyride, that I'm a coattail rider. Where does that leave me now?

I drive and drive, not knowing where I'm going. I think about what I might do with my life without him. *What can I do, what can I do?* I run through the obvious options like an old-fashioned filmstrip. I don't want to go to school; I was no good at that stuff. I don't want an office job; I had one for a short time and hated it. I can't work for somebody else; I've been working for myself, for Geoff, for way too long.

I pass an empty field, a picket fence, a row of ranch houses— and then an idea springs into my head. At Legacy Signs, we farmed out courier work every single day. We used trucking companies. We used next-day delivery. Drivers were always coming and going, picking up packages, dropping off boxes. The answer is right there under my nose, has been all along: *Why not start my own courier company? How hard can it be?*

As soon as I have this thought, I slam on the brakes. I sit there for a moment, the engine idling, marveling at the idea, then turn the car around and head straight for my parents' house.

I review the situation. Legacy used trucking companies, couriers, UPS/FedEx all the time. We had a ton of vendors to choose from and we never did it ourselves. The business opportunity seems there, and yet I have to admit that the thought of starting a courier company is a little crazy. It's a good thing I'm not in my right mind. For one thing, I don't know a lick about logistics. Heck, I don't even know my way around town. As far as business goes, the only thing I really know, when push comes to shove, is how to type. I don't know how to start a business or pay people. Yes, I helped Geoff start Legacy, but I answered the phones, filed, paid bills, and operated machinery out in the warehouse. This is a whole different kettle of fish.

I can do it, I can do it, I think, suddenly excited, suddenly clear. I have no choice but to do it. And besides, what's the worst that can happen? Anyway, I'm not going to let the worst happen. I'll prove that bastard wrong. *I don't care what it takes. He's not going to be right about me.*

Sometimes the best motivation is the desire to prove others wrong.

{ 18 }

FINGERS CROSSED

WE COULDN'T FIT one more piece of freight into our warehouse if we tried. Not even a toothpick would have slid between the wrapped pallets and boxes stacked from floor to ceiling. Our storage system, in other words, was a hot mess. To make matters worse, if a piece of freight located at the back of the building was scheduled for delivery, we'd have to empty the warehouse just to get to that one piece, drag it all out into the parking lot with forklifts, then put back each and every item. Clearly, we'd outgrown the 3,000-square-foot area mostly filled with furniture, stored there for our largest customer, but I was too nervous to move to a larger facility unless I was going to take on more work of this kind. Unless we absolutely needed it, I didn't like to spend money on anything, not even the additional warehouse space that would have made our lives that much easier. Everyone who worked with me knew this, so they'd given up grumbling about the situation, at least around me.

"Hi Michelle, my name is Jim from Teed Logistics and I'm looking for someone to service our furniture delivery work throughout New England."

I clutched the telephone. Here was another company that would need furniture storage, the one thing that would force my hand. If the fellows outside moving pallets under the hot sun knew what I was considering, they'd have jumped up and down for joy. I hesitated for a moment, then said, "We'd love to price that work out for you."

"Great," Jim said. He had a lovely, enthusiastic voice. "Before we get started, how big is your building?"

"Well, our building is a little over three thousand square feet." I envisioned this man, a complete stranger, standing before the solid mass of wood and cardboard in our warehouse, shaking his head at my having the audacity to suggest we could find a spot to store his business card, let alone his freight. What he didn't know wouldn't hurt him, however, and if he was serious about giving us the business, I could come up with a solution soon enough.

"So happens I'm traveling to Massachusetts this week and would like to see your building, if that's okay."

I was used to dealing with customers and their crazy requests. I've always said that you'd think we were delivering hearts and lungs, because everything is time critical. We once did a job for an office supply company that wanted us to deliver a case of paper towels in a nor'easter, but this situation felt far more stressful. My eyes darted back and forth as I racked my brain for a quick way out of the conundrum. One look at the current situation and Jim would turn on his heel, cursing me for wasting his precious time. That's precisely what I needed: time. Maybe I could tell him someone in my family had died, or that the State of Massachusetts had placed a ban on interstate travel, or that we planned on closing down our facility in honor of some obscure holiday—anything that would buy me a week or four. When nothing came, I tried another tactic, one that at least sounded true.

"Of course that's okay. Only thing is we're moving this weekend to a larger building. So when you come, you'll see we have no room for any more freight, but I'd be happy to show you the new space." Though I'd known we'd inevitably need a bigger space, I had yet to begin any kind of search. Finding a building with a functional warehouse wasn't like locating a new family home. You couldn't fly into the city on a Friday night, ride around the area with a realtor over the weekend, then put in an offer on Sunday evening. Now I'd have to move fast to put something in place within the next two days. Make a mistake, and I'd be paying for it for years. My hands shook from adrenaline. How on earth was I going to pull this rabbit out of the hat?

The moment I hung up, I dragged out the phone book, flipped it open on my cluttered desk, and located several commercial realtors. I called them one by one to inquire after any available space for lease. While each prepared a list for me, a process that could take an hour or days for all I knew, I jumped in my car and drove around the area in search of industrial parks to see if anyone had a For Rent sign on their front lawn. Up one street and down the other I crept, like a cat burglar.

Finally, I stumbled across an industrial park in Randolph. There, before a worn-out row of juniper bushes, stood the sign I had been looking for. Eyeing the building, I determined it was the size I wanted, with good loading access. Trucks could pull in and on- or off-load with relative ease. The location was good as well. I called the management company listed on the sign to see if I could get in to see it.

A couple of minutes later, an agent called me back and gave me the details of the building, and told me I could see it the next day if I wanted. I sat in the car, my hands resting on the steering wheel, and studied the building some more, contemplating the downside. We'd be paying a lot more for space than I'd ever paid before. What happened if I took the place on and didn't land this new piece of business? I'd be on the hook for a multiyear lease and would have to lay people off just to cover my exposure. Maybe it would get so bad I'd wind up back in the laundry room, fighting bankruptcy. The building was in Randolph, as opposed to Braintree, where we currently were; maybe the location wasn't so perfect after all. Maybe moving to Randolph from Braintree portended disaster. What if we lost our Braintree phone number and our customers couldn't reach us? We were on their speed dial. If the number didn't ring through, they'd press another number, a competitor's number, rather than look us up. Or what if our current phone number was composed of lucky numbers. One change in the sequence and we'd throw off the stars responsible for keeping us afloat. Because seriously, luck, fate, angels—*whatever*—had to be what kept this business growing. Why mess with the formula? That phone number, like my decades-old calculator, symbolized my independence, freedom from the past; I had no interest in letting it slip from my grip.

I met the broker the following morning and he gave me a tour of the building. "This is what we're looking for," I told him, "and I'd be interested in taking it." I explained that I needed to discuss the details with my office manager and that I'd get back to him in a day. Mind you, I didn't need to discuss the details or the decision with anyone, but I did need to stall. Was Jim, the promising new customer, really on his way? Were we really in the running for this work, or had someone else landed the business in the twenty-four-hour interim? Why move, why risk messing with the stars, if I didn't have to?

Jim called the next day to report that he was in town and that he'd like to visit both my current and new locations. My palms immediately began to sweat. "Of course," I said to him, throwing in a breezy laugh for good measure. My mind raced, a spastic greyhound going round and round the track. *What am I going to do?*!

I phoned the broker and asked if I could see the new space again. Not wanting anyone to meet me there, because Jim thought the building was mine, I explained that I didn't know what time I'd be there. Instead of having someone wait around, I proposed, why not leave the door unlocked? I did my best to sound calm, sensible, anything that would belie the fact that I was out of my mind and doing my darnedest to cover up a bold-faced lie so I could save my dignity and win the new business. Well, maybe it wasn't really a lie. I did have plans to move— eventually. I crossed my fingers and toes, even my eyes. "Please, please, please," I chanted under my breath.

"Sure," the broker said.

I stared at the phone receiver in my hand, shook my head in wonderment. I couldn't believe I was actually going to pull this caper off.

When Jim arrived the following day, as promised, I gave him a tour of our current location. He took one look at the state of our warehouse, brushed his dark hair back with one hand, and laughed. "Well, I can see why you need a change of venue. You're moving this weekend, right?"

I laughed as if he'd just said the craziest thing.

We headed over to the new location. At each stoplight, I assured him that we were moving, that I was excited about the move, that my people were all but packed and on their way out the door, like a line of worker ants. That it would take us a week or so to settle, and everyone was really excited, and... I knew I was talking too much, but I couldn't stop.

The door of the new building was open. I breathed a sigh of relief, having imagined myself breaking a back window and crawling through glass shards to let us in. "You know how we women are," I would have said, slapping my forehead, "always losing our keys at the bottom of some handbag. Silly, silly me." I found the light switch, flicked it on, and conducted the tour, highlighting the massive warehouse floor. Jim smiled, infinitely satisfied.

For whatever reason, I didn't land Jim's business. When I heard the news a week after his visit, I sat in my Braintree office considering my options. I no longer had to move, given the disappointing circumstances, but I knew that if I didn't, I'd be right back in this ridiculous position the next time a big customer looked my way. I might be able to pull off that kind of charade once, but I wouldn't be able to do it again. I could hear the forklifts out in the parking lot, the beeping as one of them backed up. I laughed because, really, we were bursting at the seams and going to ridiculous lengths to disguise that fact. But then I went quiet. Moving without the business to cover the lease—that was a real risk. There was a lot at stake. My livelihood and sense of accomplishment were on the line, but more importantly, I had a lot of people depending on me for a paycheck. I had loyal customers I didn't want to let down.

I took a deep breath, closed my eyes for a minute, then reached for the phone. There's never a good time to buy a house, never a good time to get married, never a good time to have a baby. Why was this situation any different? I dialed the broker before I could chicken out. "We're going to take the building," I told him. "Draw up the paperwork."

A few months after moving into our Braintree location, I heard a rumor. Jim had lost his delivery contract. He no longer needed the storage capacity or the associated delivery services. The competitor who had won his nightmarish business was stuck holding the bag.

The what-ifs can kill you if you let them. They can block your momentum and keep you small.

_____

{ 19 }

GEOFF RETURNS

ONE AFTERNOON, just as I'm getting home from work, I hear the apartment phone ringing. I run up the stairs as fast as I can. I unlock the front door, race to the kitchen, and answer. "Hey, why are you out of breath?" Geoff says.

It's the first time I've heard his voice since the day I collected my things at Legacy. A string of conflicting emotions, one after the other, hit me in the throat: surprise, anger, joy, hope, and then wariness. I tell him I'm not out of breath, as though he's honed in on another of my many weaknesses that he can manipulate, and ask why he's calling.

"Just checking on you. Seeing what you've been up to."

I tell him I'm well, that I've been keeping busy, going out with my friends, which is a total lie. I work eighteen hours a day; they go out clubbing while I sleep. Yes, I'm doing better, but definitely not as well as I'm making it sound. The thought of him laughing at how lame my life is without him, of giving him the tiniest taste of satisfaction, makes me turn up the energy in my voice.

I want to sound as if I'm cartwheeling through life, drinking endless piña coladas with beautiful, fun-loving people. On top of the world. If he knows I don't need him to be happy, he'll want me more. If he knows other people value my company, he'll treat me better when we get back together.

He makes small talk while I wait for the punch line. He's done this hundreds of times: break up with me then call me back when his latest relationship goes south, when he realizes that there's nothing better out there. I can recite the script nearly word for word. I'll come running the second I hang up the phone—that's the next line of this play.

Finally, he asks, "So, you want to meet for a drink?"

I clutch one of the chairs to steady myself. The wood feels smooth and cool.

A piece of me thinks, *Yes, I want to go out for a drink! Yes, yes, YES!* I open my mouth to say, "Sure, that'd be great," but the words that come out are, "No, I can't meet you."

I stop talking and blink at the wall in front of me. Where did that come from? I look down at my shaking body from above—is that possible?—and marvel at the words this girl has just spoken. My mouth moves, my lips form the syllables and consonants, but that's not my voice speaking. It's far too casual and self-assured, uninterested even.

"What do you mean?" he says.

I tell him once again that I'm not going to meet him. I go numb so I no longer feel surprised by my words, no longer float above my own head like a disembodied spirit. Taken off guard, what with me deviating from the script, he hesitates, and then changes the subject. "So, what have you been up to?"

"I started my own business." I'm not sure if I'm telling him this by way of an explanation or if I want to stick it to him, to prove to him that I can be more than fine without him, that I can be successful on my own. He isn't the brain and brawn behind it all, as he claimed; I am. *Tell me I'll never amount to anything without you, I'll show you.* Part of me wants to puff out my chest; the other part knows this is the quickest way to draw Geoff's fire.

"Oh, you started that because of me," he says with a dismissive laugh. "I take credit for that."

I hang on the other end of the line and take in his comment. Try as I might, I can't wrap my head around his arrogance, his desire to rob me of any pride. I was good to him. I loved him blindly. I forgave him the curses and punches and nonstop put-downs. I forgave him the torment he thrived on. Can't he give me this? After a moment, I hang up the phone.

A week or so later, Geoff calls again, this time at my office in my parents' house. I can't believe he found my office number, that he took the time to track it down. "So, this is your new business?" he asks as if surveying the pool table; the washing machine and dryer; the files stacked on the linoleum floor; my high heels, which to him would only appear pathetic.

"Yes, I started a courier service." I try to sound confident.

He laughs. I can picture him sitting in his office chair, throwing his head back, his mouth open wide. "You know nothing about the industry."

"You're right, I don't, but I'll make it work." I have no choice but to make it work because there's no way in hell I'm going to prove Geoff right.

"Well, I have a shipment I can use you for, and a couple customers I can use you for." He's dangling a carrot, seeing if the promise of a little money, some easy business, will get me in the door. Once I'm in the door, I'm his to do with as he pleases. He knows it, and so do I.

I've always known that if I want my business to be successful—if I wanted to be infinitely successful from day one, from the second that phone jack was plugged in—all I have to do is call him. He can feed me more work than I know what to do with.

His account would be a guaranteed stream of work and cash as well. And I've always known that he'd give me that work. He kicked me to the curb with nothing, and giving it to me would be just the thing to let him off the hook.

When I don't respond, Geoff asks me again, "So, do you want some work?"

I could make so much money and do away with all of the stress and crying. I could operate in the black with enough money to go shopping, and I love shopping, I miss shopping. I want pretty dresses, high heels, and jewelry. I want the works. And I want time to myself, to be able to go out with my friends and family, not to bail every single time a customer calls. I don't want to hit the industrial parks and strip malls day after day looking for business, dealing with constant rejection, which is precisely what's required to keep the lights on.

That dangling carrot looks delicious, but I also know it's deadly poisonous. I can't do that to myself. I won't do that to myself. I know that the day I take a job from Geoff, he'll own me again. And—just like he's doing anyway—he'll take credit for my success. He'll tell everyone that he helped me start my company, and if I take work from him, that will be true. I'm not about to let that happen. I know it means taking the hard road, but at least my business will be mine. My road. I can take any direction I want. He won't control it. So I reply, "No, thank you."

He seems surprised. "What do you mean, no thank you?"

"I mean, I won't do your work."

All the blood, sweat, and tears from sitting on that bumper pool table, flipping through that phone book and calling customer after customer, getting rejection after rejection—all of the discomfort and endless uncertainty that have made me who I am will be for nothing if I take this job from Geoff. Everything that he's ever said about me will be true. I would rather cry myself a river, deliver packages that weigh more than me, and have zero life for another ten years than be the person he claims I am—stupid, worthless, weak, a leech, a hanger-on. Nothing good can possibly come from a deal with the devil.

*Don't avoid the hard road.
That's the road that will
make you who you are.*

{ 20 }

THE BIG DIG

I WAS AT AN emergency meeting of industry leaders when the topic of joining forces came up. Ever since the State of Massachusetts had made it illegal for businesses of any kind to use independent contractors—a knee-jerk response to lost tax revenue during the Big Dig, a huge construction project that nearly bankrupted the state, involving thousands of undocumented illegal immigrants paid under the table—we courier owners were all sitting ducks. Knowing that I'd grown a strong business over the course of more than twenty years, and that I was active and engaged in the community, as well as a sucker for hard work, somebody asked me if I would resurrect the Massachusetts Delivery Association (MDA), an old organization that had all but died, and serve as its president. I looked around at the nervous people in the room. These were my competitors, many of whom I considered friends. Some were in the middle of lawsuits that would cost them millions; others were facing the likelihood of the same.

The Attorney General's office, which was in charge of cracking down on anyone who refused to obey this new law, didn't intend to go after every industry that used independent contractors; they had bigger fish to fry, namely the construction industry, particularly those involved in the Big Dig. But then a wily lawyer saw a loophole in this new, convoluted law and decided to target courier companies because of our business model, which has always been based on independent contractors—hundreds of thousands of independent contractors. He essentially hunted for drivers who were willing to sue a company, so both the driver and the lawyer could make a ton of money.

Suddenly, drivers began to wield major power. File one complaint, and a courier company faced a major investigation by the Attorney General's office and a potential lawsuit. Because of the associated fines and legal expenses, these drivers, with the help of the wily attorney, realized that it would be less expensive for a company to settle than to fight the complainant in court. And at the end of the day, it was almost impossible for a courier company to win in court.

All of this began to get very expensive. Companies were settling class actions for hundreds of thousands of dollars, some of the larger ones in the millions. A driver would see the kind of money the others were getting and decide to put his own hand into the cookie jar. As big as this industry was and is, we all pulled from the same circle of drivers, and these drivers had become sue-happy. It was only a matter of time before some unscrupulous driver took another one of us out.

I felt awful for those at the meeting. One owner, who'd been through the wringer with a driver I knew, looked as though he'd aged ten years. Another was poised to sell his company for pennies on the dollar because he'd never recover from the fleecing. Without thinking, I said I would lead the fight by taking on the role of president of the association, even though I knew nothing about legal nuance, or how to fight the law. I was willing to figure it out as I went along, and that was all that seemed to be required. I'd come this far on a wing and a prayer, so why not carry on? No one else seemed to have a solution; no one else wanted to lead the charge.

I surrounded myself with extremely knowledgeable people, and together we formed a solid yet small group. We quickly determined that we needed more people to help the cause, but as big as the courier industry was, everybody seemed to have gone to ground. Not a lot of companies wanted to be associated with the MDA lest the wily attorney got a hold of the list of participating courier companies and went after them. There our small group was, red capes flapping in the wind, tempting the bull to charge at us.

We also realized that we needed money to hire a lobbyist to fight on our behalf, to get as much current information as possible from the state Senate floor regarding this law so that we could have some effect. An adviser to the group determined that it would be wise to go after some language in the law—replace an "or" with an "and"—that would allow the continued use of independent contractors.

We tried to get the law changed, and get the nuanced language changed, but we quickly realized it would be next to impossible. Each of our recommendations was vetoed. (It's very difficult to get a law changed regardless of what that law is.)

After a year of continual battle, we decided that the best way to put an end to this harassment and highway robbery was to sue the State of Massachusetts.

Sitting in my home office, I talked with the lead labor law attorney the group had hired, while my kids ran in and out, chasing after our barking dog.

"I believe you guys can win this case," he said. "It's going to take a while to fight it. It's going to take a lot of money to fight it. You'll need to get this association up and running properly, or you'll be too weak to fight. We want to help you with it, and I think we can be successful."

The man seemed confident, completely centered despite the household chaos swirling around us. I toyed with the old calculator that lived on my desk. One of the kids shrieked with laughter from the kitchen.

The lawyer outlined his plan of attack. We'd need to present a test case to the court, which would demonstrate how the courier business model worked. We reviewed a number of different companies, looking to see who would best represent us, but most of them were not in a strong-enough position to do so. The suit would be lost before we started.

The lawyer asked me to be the test case, to represent all of the courier owners.

I leaned back in my chair and studied the ceiling. I was due to be married in a couple of weeks, having been single since my divorce. I'd found a great guy, one I could trust; now I was about to throw a wrench into the works. As it was, I already felt over-extended when it came to my home life. I'd been one step ahead of my kids for years, forever making business deals while they tried to get my attention. Half the time I had to hole up in the car out in the driveway to get a minute or two of quiet, just so I could close an important deal or hash out a contract. In the driver's seat, I'd stick a piece of paper up against the window so I couldn't see their little faces. At least one of the two would be crying, pounding on the window, wanting me, Mother of the Year, to referee their fight or solve some issue. Now I was being asked to take on something that would take an inordinate amount of my energy, bandwidth, and time.

"This is going to be a lot on the family," my fiancé said when I broached the subject that evening. "You're already stressed out as it is. Xpressman's name isn't out there. You've never had a lawsuit against your company. You don't have anybody mad at you. You'll be exposing yourself unnecessarily."

I took a sip of wine and closed my eyes. It was only a matter of time before some driver came after my company. You didn't need to be Oda Mae to see that coming. "If we don't face fear head-on, then we're going to be waiting for the other shoe to drop from here on in." I remembered the FBI knocking at my door years before, taking me to task on workers' comp issues, showing me how easily I could be brought to my knees when I least expected it. At this stage of the game, no one would shake his head at my naïveté or go easy on me. As the head of a successful courier company, I had no excuse and a lot more to lose. I weighed all the considerations of serving as the test case. I ran a reasonably "clean" company because I'd learned the ropes the hard way. I followed the independent contractor rules. Drivers came and went as they pleased; they had to work for other businesses, not just mine. I didn't do a lot of the things that other courier companies did that confused the "independent contractor versus employee" issue, or that brought lawsuits against them.

Nobody would serve as the perfect test case; I knew it and so did the attorney, but I was as close as we were going to get. A judge would likely find me sympathetic. I was a woman operating in a highly competitive, predominantly male industry, and had been for over twenty years. My company wasn't the largest, nor was it the smallest. I had a compelling story to tell. Most people in positions of power were willing to help the hard-working underdog, which is what I'd always been.

I agreed to be the test case despite the sinking feeling I was about to get in way over my head. It was going to be the Massachusetts Delivery Association versus the State, but really, it was going to be Xpressman versus the Attorney General, David versus Goliath. Mother Mary, let me come out on top.

It was a crazy amount of work to take on, even by my standards. In the thick of it, I was deposed twice, and let me tell you, it's brutal to be the subject of a deposition. The only things missing from the experience were bright lights shining in my eyes, water dripping on my forehead, and someone ripping my fingernails out. I had to produce over one hundred thousand pages for the court; nothing was too private.

The legal expenses were covered by the MDA, but those funds were drying up quickly because several members had reneged on their promise to pay their dues.

We held an emergency meeting to discuss the court case. A number of folks who had failed to pay their dues were present, gathering free information so they could stay out of trouble.

I was shaking; my heart was racing. I kept rehearsing the speech I planned to give, the one that would inspire everybody to donate so we could win the war. Once they'd heard my story—how I'd scratched my way to where I was now, sacrificed my personal life, dealt with constantly changing regulations and crazy drivers and employees looking to take advantage of me, harass me—I knew they would. Nobody had handed me anything, and yet here I was, willing to give it all, even after spending an unjustifiable amount of time fighting for the cause, our cause.

The meeting was almost done when our lawyer said, "Okay, anybody have any questions?"

"You know what? Actually, I do," I said, getting up. I grabbed the microphone from his hand and proceeded to pace around the room. "I know all of you know who I am. I'm Michelle Cully, owner of Xpressman. But I don't think you all know the story behind my business. Let me tell you. I started a business..."

When I was wrapping it up, I said, "You all sit there and you hide, and you don't pay your dues. You leave it up to us—the same people, right here in this row, Steve, Eric, Fred, Aaron, and myself—to fight for this cause, to fund it, while you all hide behind the rocks." I looked one of the guilty parties—a middle-aged man I knew to have deep pockets—right in the eye. "I'm the one that isn't able to go out and build my business and make it what I should be making it, or what I could be making it, because I'm here fighting this case, because I'm the one being deposed, because I'm the one pulling out document after document and presenting them to the court. That's what I'm doing.

"And why am I doing this? Who am I doing this for? I'm doing it for every single one of you." I pointed at an owner who had inherited his business from his father, who had promised to pay his dues six months running but never had. "So while you sit there and say you're going to pay, you should be paying, because this is for you, and it's for your future, for your kids' future, for your grandchildren's future. It's not for me, it's for everybody."

When I'd said my piece, the audience members stood and applauded, even the ones who hadn't paid. I set the microphone down on one of the folding chairs. People sidled up to me and said, "I wish you'd YouTubed that. I wish you'd share that message with other associations. We would really get a lot of money in. It was incredible."

I'd never considered myself the strong one. Sure, I'd been willing to take a risk when my back was up against the wall, when I could see no other way out, but for once I realized that no one had more guts than Michelle Cully. I was the one who made things happen; the rest, with few exceptions, were hangers-on.

WE LOST THE first round of the test case. I was gutted, but pressed on, taking the case to the Court of Appeals and having it reinstated.

Shortly thereafter, I was served with a misclassification suit.

The wily attorney who was suing on behalf of the drivers had gotten a hold of James, an independent contractor I'd used a year and a half before—or James had gotten a hold of the attorney. James was claiming he'd been hired as an employee, not an independent contractor. He knew how easy it was to shake down any company in the industry—everyone did.

Once again it was me who showed up in court, answered all of the questions about my company, provided countless documents plus our policies and procedures. I was grilled on each and every line item, day after day after day.

At night, lying awake, I wondered why I'd ever agreed to be the test case, why I'd bothered to put myself through it all. My fiancé, who was now my husband, had warned me that I would only bring trouble down on my head, and from all appearances he'd been right. We'd lost round one of the test case suit, and we all knew there'd be more. We lost the next round, took it to the Court of Appeals, then got the case reinstated again, then finally won. We obtained a first-of-its-kind ruling that independent contractor laws like the one Massachusetts has are unconstitutional, as they relate to couriers. And the wave of lawsuits against courier companies has broken and receded. But I wasn't done, not by a long shot. On top of all that, I now had my own lawsuit to deal with thanks to James.

But then I thought about why I was doing it all. By winning the case, I proved to everybody that I have a very solid company indeed. That I created all of this despite some jerk telling me I'd never amount to anything without him.

Sometimes it's the mouse who helps the lion, not the other way around.

{ 21 }

I DON'T CARE

I DON'T HEAR FROM Geoff for months, though I keep expecting the phone to ring with another job offer, another invitation to grab a drink. I know he's out there, just waiting to come at me from another angle, to approach when I'm far more vulnerable. But in the end it isn't Geoff who calls me; it's the other way around. When I hear that he's dating the same girl he tended to go back to whenever he broke up with me, I lunge for the phone, outraged and out of control, and call him.

"Are you kidding me? You're dating *her*? You're dating *her*?!" He can't get a word in edgewise, I'm screaming so much. Then I hang up on him and fling myself face-first onto Gina's couch, where I still sleep each night.

I'm ready to cry the way I always have when Geoff and I got into it, but nothing comes. I think of the worst thing he's ever said or done to me, but I can't force the tears. I picture them together, making mad, passionate love on some tropical beach, him calling her "baby" and "love of my life." His hands on her thighs, her lips on his neck. Nothing.

That's when Shea walks through the front door. I say to her, "I'm so mad. I'm so depressed." I explain what's just happened, what Geoff has gone and done, my puzzling lack of tears.

Shea grins. She jumps onto the couch beside me and examines my face. Were she the affectionate sort, she'd stroke my face. Instead, she laughs at me because she can tell I'm fake crying, and not very well.

"You were just trying to force a cry and you couldn't do it! You don't care if he's dating her. You really don't care. It doesn't even bother you, so get over it." She says this as if it's a really happy thing.

I argue back. "It bothers me! I care!" Even then I can't offer a single tear of proof.

It was Shea who gave me Louise the cat for my sixteenth birthday. I was allergic to cats—well, I thought I was at the time—but Shea didn't care. "You're not funny," I told her. "This is not a cool joke." She said, "I'm not kidding. I asked your parents if I could give you one and they said I could." She had some nerve, asking my parents if she could give me a pet. Of course, as soon as I picked Louise up, it was love at first sight for both of us. I suppose Shea knew that would be the case.

"Michelle, face it, you don't even care," she says now.

I stop for a minute and think about what she's just said. I feel around inside myself for some emotion, any emotion, and I realize I *don't* care. I do *not* care. I don't care!

I start laughing too. It's such a relief. I just lie there, with the hung-up phone next to me, belly-laughing. Then I stop for a moment and say to Shea, "You're right. I don't care about him. I don't care if he marries her. He's gross to me. He's gross inside and out. Oh my God, I don't care!"

I'm free.

Sometimes you just let go.

_____

EPILOGUE

A COUPLE OF PEOPLE told me that I should end this book with my husband and I marrying and sailing off into the sunset. Umm, no. First, we don't own a sailboat and neither of us knows how to sail. Second, I hardly ever see the sunset because I'm in bed too early. Third, sailing into the sunset wouldn't work, not the way it does in the movies, because no sooner would we push off from the dock than we'd have to make pit stops to drop my daughter off at riding, my son at his singing lessons, all while the two of us were on the phone dealing with a million different work issues. Mugzy the dog would also be there, swimming behind the boat, barking like a fool, because God forbid he be left alone for a second.

I raise an eyebrow whenever people say their significant other completes them, or that their world would be nothing without him or her. Really? How could someone have those kinds of thoughts? Don't get me wrong: I love my husband, and it doesn't mean that I love him less because I don't believe he completes me. If you were to ask him, he would tell you that I don't complete him either. I know that he loves me. You can meet the person you're supposed to love, be happy with him or her, make memories together, but you complete yourself. You should never depend on anyone to do that for you. If Geoff taught me anything, it's that.

We all make our own happiness. We can't always control our own misery, we all get handed our trials, but we can control our happiness. If you wait for someone to complete you or wait for someone to make you happy, you may be waiting a lifetime—and who has time for that?

I know how easy it is to turn over the controls to someone else, to think he's going to do it all for you, make your dreams come true. That mistake nearly killed me.

Do not relinquish the controls. It's all on you, babe.

If there's one thing you can depend on in this life, it's change. It can work for you or against you; much of that is up to you.

If I lose one client, I'll work to replace it with another. I'm constantly looking for ways to diversify and grow my business so I'm not stuck; I refuse to succumb to fate, or an underhanded employee, or a change in the law. I know when a type of business is going to dry up, which customers won't likely be there anymore because of changes in the market, and I start to diversify my clientele. I study the signs and I know their meaning. I won't make that mistake ever again, sticking my head in the sand and hoping the problem corrects itself. It's been hard, because some of these niches have been extremely profitable, but then that kind of business doesn't really exist anymore, and those profit margins dry up. I've always had to find ways to stay ahead of the times and changes in technology, to prepare to lose one type of client or gain another.

I know I'm an entrepreneur because that's what entrepreneurs do: they roll with changes. I know I've grown up because that's what adults do: they deal with challenges head-on. They pull their own poker out of the fire.

I've always been stressed about work, but I've learned to go with the flow. I don't second-guess myself. I go full force, never look back, never doubt myself, and I make major decisions that could affect a lot of people.

The flipside is in my personal life. I can't make a decision to save my life. I'll go through every paint shade in the Benjamin Moore wheel because I can't pick out a color for my kitchen. I can't decide on a couch. Everything I buy, I end up returning.

I've always said that I run my business like a pro and my personal life, well, that's where I fall down on the job. I've made the worst choices in my personal life, and it's so funny because my friends will ask me why I can't run my private life the way I run my business. But truly, it's been a struggle.

The one saving grace is that I've learned to speak up about the things that matter. I don't run from a confrontation the way I used to. I've learned not to say, "It's okay. Next time." In the past, I would've acquiesced to keep the peace with my partner. "Sure, I can buy lunch all week on $1.95," when I have a $10 daily allowance. I've used that strategy in business to my advantage, dialing my agenda back for the greater good, but that doesn't work at home. Acquiesce all the time and you'll lose yourself; you'll forget who you are and what you really want. I stay away from that stuff because it's a slippery slope. I'm pretty fond of having an identity, and I refuse to give that up just to please somebody.

I look back and I remember being attracted to Geoff because he was the kind of guy who could take us places—charismatic, from a wealthy family, hardworking, a go-getter. I wanted to be a millionaire by the time I was thirty, and with him I figured it was bound to happen. But I ended up doing that on my own.

I've seen from afar what Geoff has accomplished, and he's done well for himself. He deserves success because he's always worked for it. I can't take that away from him, regardless of our insane history. But I have him to thank, in many ways, for my own success. He lit a fire under my ass, a desire to prove him wrong, even if that wasn't his intention, and that's just what I did.

I make great money, but there's a price to pay for that. I'd love to take a step back. I don't always want to keep going at this pace. I want to be able to slow down long enough to enjoy the fruits of my labor.

Joy is spending time with the kids, whether it's going out for an ice cream or taking them on a ski trip to France. It wasn't until I met my current husband that I started to travel. I never really had anyone to travel with, on the rare occasions I could step away from the business for longer than fifteen minutes. I'd hardly ever, in over twenty years of business, had a real vacation. I'd been away; I'd been out of the country; I'd been to Germany and Austria and Italy, sure, but I always had to work. I'd never had a true vacation, where I had my phone off, no access. Now that I'm traveling more, enjoying this other life, I'm discovering that there are such incredible experiences in this world. That's what success means to me, not just the balance in my bank accounts.

Success for me also means having a nice house in a good neighborhood. When I pull into that driveway, I think, *I built that house at thirty-four years old. That's my gift to myself. That's the embodiment of my accomplishment.*

Now what gives me great pleasure is decorating that house. I think of all those fun things I missed out on while I was up to my eyeballs in deliveries—nightclubbing with the girls, trips to Barbados with my sister and Shea, dinners with my family without having to break away for some emergency or other. This is the way I've rewarded myself. And dressing nicely. These are the things that make me happy. Making a cup of tea and sitting in the corner of my room and looking at my house and saying, "Oh my God, I love it." That makes me happy.

Xpressman Trucking and Courier Inc. is 24/7, 365 days a year. Drivers go out throughout the night and day. The only time I don't work, or can take a breath, is from Sunday around 2 p.m. until Monday morning. That's truly the only time I'm not worried about something in the business, or that I won't get an emergency phone call, or occasionally have to dispatch a job to a driver.

I do so many different things that it's hard to say what I do exactly. I'm in charge of everyone who works here. Even though employees and contractors report to different people, at the end of the day I'm the one whom everybody comes to. I'm the one who deals with the more demanding customers and who runs the numbers on my trusty calculator. I love bringing the work in. My adrenaline pumping, I have no idea how we're gonna get it done, but I'll do anything to make it happen. I'll sweep floors and take out the trash. Exhausting or not, you've just got to do what it takes—that's how you get ahead. You're never able to rest. But it's worth it, it really is.

"You have no idea how much you've inspired me," someone will say when I give a speech. "I've been wanting to open my own business for ages." They look at me for encouragement, as if I can get them moving. Sometimes I think I'd do them a great service by giving them the once-over, sneering, and saying, "You'll never amount to anything, that much is clear to me." But I'm too nice a person.

I want to say, "The problems you worry about aren't the ones that take you down anyway. So why not do what you want to do and get on with it already?" Instead, I say, "People always say, 'It's not a good time, so I'll have to do it later.' Well, when is it a good time? Truly, when is it the right time to start anything that matters, that requires you to risk?" Their hesitation seems funny to me, but then I remember it's easier to see a situation for what it is when you've got some distance. I see that the thing they want so badly, but that they're also so afraid of, could be the best thing for them.

There have been times in my life when an opportunity has come my way, when somehow the thing felt right, and I've thought, *I'm going to go with it, I'm going to do it. I don't have a business plan. I don't know what's going to happen tomorrow, let alone five years from now. But I just have to go with it.* And that's how you do this stuff, whether you have an Oda Mae sixth sense or not. You take a chance, you take a risk, and you work to make it happen. You don't give up, and you remember that you've got yourself to do right by. That's how you grow up, make something of yourself, get what you want.

If I could do it with very little money, zero self-esteem, and no plan whatsoever, what excuse does anyone else have?

BONUS LESSONS

Do not suffer analysis paralysis.

START SMALL AND build until you can't get any higher. Set yourself up for success by taking small steps that will get you to your goal.

Monitor your control center.

OWNING YOUR OWN business is a lot like being a pilot: you have all the control and, in the event that something goes wrong, you're responsible. The good news is that you can also control what you delegate—and delegate you must. Micromanaging will kill your business and your personal life.

Trust your gut—in relationships and in business.

I'VE SPENT MY life being so afraid of conflict that I ignored what I knew to be the right thing to do. The fear of confrontation won over my very strong intuition. I was so afraid to do the wrong thing and piss anyone off that I became a yes-person, never wanting to disappoint. Look where that got me in my relationships. My gut has always done right by me, and now I know when I'm ignoring it. I still hate confrontation, but I understand that my gut knows better.

Opportunity is always ringing. Answer.

IF YOU THOUGHT long and hard on what you were about to do, you'd never have the courage to do it. Opportunity is not always going to plop itself in front of you in a nicely wrapped box with an instruction letter on how to proceed. Sometimes opportunity arrives at a low time in your life. Sometimes opportunity forces you out of your comfort zone. Sometimes just getting out of your comfort zone and saying, "Screw it, let's see what this is all about," can open amazing doors.

Failure is not
a four-letter word.

WE OFTEN BEAT ourselves up over mistakes when what we need to do is embrace them, learn from them, and then grow from them. Failing is part of life; quitting because things are too hard is not okay. There were times in my career when I wanted to give up and give in. But I didn't, and that was by choice. Every time I was faced with the unknown, I tackled it head-on, because nobody was going to do it for me. Don't wait for perfection, because you'll be waiting forever. Get out there, make a few mistakes, and learn from them.

The smartest thing you
can do is surround yourself
with smarty-pants.

LEADERS ARE ONLY as good as the people they surround themselves with. Listen to them, learn from them, then repeat the process.

Material objects don't fill the empty space in your heart.

SURE, I LOVE my house and possessions, but I measure my success by the level of my passion, the happiness of my children, and the contribution I make to the world. When I go to bed each night, I remind myself that I've done the very best I could for that day. I've tried to be a good leader, a good thinker, a mentor, and a loving mom. That, to me, is the measure of success.

Love and friendship never come with a price tag.

YOU CAN'T BUY love. You can't give everything you've got—time, money, focus, and energy—in exchange for adoration. That kind of "love" is cheap and never lasts. That strategy places you in a powerless position, one that's ripe for abuse.

Give with no expectations of getting.

IF YOU GIVE a compliment, don't expect one back; do it because you mean it. If you give a donation, don't expect recognition; do it because you're passionate about the cause. Having expectations that the world works "tit for tat" will always leave you feeling cheated. Do because you feel great doing.

Show grace under pressure.

IN THE PAST, I would react automatically to a situation, which caused me to make bad decisions. When you stop to listen and truly think through the situation, it gives you time to process, digest, and then respond.

Express gratitude when it's been earned.

WHEN YOU ACKNOWLEDGE someone, be it an employee or a family member, and express gratitude, it makes that person feel proud and validated. We tend to focus on what people do wrong instead of praising them for what they've done right. Let's switch that up.

Busy doesn't mean productive.

YOU CAN STAY busy doing nothing all day. Over the years, I've had to become more organized in order to become more productive. I can't count the number of hours I've murdered looking for an e-mail, trying to remember the time of my next conference call, and so on. A good friend of mine gave me the simplest advice: "Michelle, you need to create a To-Do List, and work your way through that list every day." I know this sounds pretty basic, but sometimes it's the basics we need to learn most.

Speak often;
listen more.

ASK WHEN YOU have a question and zip it when you have nothing to say. It really is that easy. You can learn an awful lot about yourself and the world by listening to other people's viewpoints without struggling to weigh in.

If it were easy, everyone
would be doing it.

FOR YEARS, I kept this saying in my wallet. I would take out the note and read it periodically when the going got tough. If the easy road is what you expect, then expect to be underwhelmed.

Always stay humble and kind.

(THANKS, TIM MCGRAW, for the song with these lyrics.) I've stayed very humble throughout my career. I've worked hard and under the radar for so long. It took me decades before I could bring myself to put the word "President" on my business cards; it felt braggy. Humble, however, doesn't mean weak. Kind doesn't make you a pushover. Some of the kindest people I know are tough as nails. Humble and kind just means you want good for others and you don't judge.

If you don't believe in you, no one else will either.

WHEN WE TRY to be something we're not, we just look and sound like frauds. When I was first asked to do a commencement speech, I wrote what I thought was some pretty good stuff. I quoted philosophers, civil rights leaders, professors, and so on. I thought I sounded brilliant—except I didn't. My speechwriter made me cut out the "smart" stuff and tell my own truth. It was great advice, because instead of quoting someone I'd never read, I simply told my own story. My audience appreciated my honesty. Only when I realized my own truth was enough were others able to recognize the same.

ACKNOWLEDGMENTS

THANK YOU TO Xpressman for giving me a reason to get up and put on my high heels, and for supplying a purpose when I didn't think I had one.

Thank you to my amazing children. You are my world and my life. I love you.

Thank you to my husband for knowing how important it is for me to tell my story. I love you.

Thank you to my parents for their unconditional love, my dad's shoulder, and my mom's determination.

Thank you to my siblings. You have been by my side through this journey without any judgment, just love and support.

Thank you to all my sisters- and brothers-in-law for all your support.

Thank you, Kelly. Who would have thought a standby would have changed the course of my journey?

Father Kelly, thank you for being there and letting me cry. Mother Mary, thank you for placing your hands on top of mine.

Susan, thank you for listening when at times I wasn't even talking. Anna, thank you for letting me find my voice. MJE, thank you for hearing my voice.

Gail, Mom, Gina, and Auntie Patsy, thank you for picking me up and moving me out. If you hadn't, I'd still be lying on the floor.

Thank you to Brookes and Ann for helping me tell my story. KDaly, thank you for being there to help me tell my story out loud. Thank you to all my friends and loved ones—you know who you are! A big thank you to Indiana: I found the love...

Thank you to Kerry for helping me nail the cover photo.

Thank you, Elisha and Olivia, for styling me in ways I never could.

Thank you to Kristin for designing the laundry room of my dreams.

Thank you to Page Two for believing in this project, Trena, Amanda, and the whole team. I knew it was a good fit when we all cried during our first meeting!